Belfast
WALKS

Seth Linder

A Londoner by birth, Seth Linder has lived in Northern Ireland for over twenty years. He is a journalist, author and scriptwriter. He has been involved in numerous projects exploring the heritage, history and culture of Belfast, including Belfast City Hall's centenary exhibition and the award-winning 'Belfast Bred' dramatised food tour of the city, produced by Kabosh Theatre. Working with local historians and community groups throughout Belfast, Seth has gained a unique insight into the city's communities and areas. He scripted the groundbreaking iTours video guides to Belfast and a series of booklets covering the city's arts and cultural scenes. Seth is the author of *Ripper Diary: The Inside Story*, published by Sutton Publishing Ltd.

Belfast

WALKS

Seth Linder

THE O'BRIEN PRESS
DUBLIN

First published 2018 by The O'Brien Press Ltd,

12 Terenure Road East, Rathgar, Dublin 6, D06 HD27, Ireland.

Tel: +353 1 4923333; Fax: +353 1 4922777

E-mail: books@obrien.ie; Website: www.obrien.ie

The O'Brien Press is a member of Publishing Ireland.

ISBN: 978-1-84717-925-8

Every effort has been made to trace copyright holders and to obtain their permission for the use of copyright material. The publisher apologises for any errors or omissions and would be grateful if notified of any corrections that should be incorporated in future reprints or editions of this book.

10 9 8 7 6 5 4 3 2 1

23 22 21 20 19 18

Printed and bound in Poland by Białostockie Zakłady Graficzne S.A.

The paper in this book is produced using pulp from managed forests.

Published in

Dedication

To Deirdre, Conor, Ciara, Saoirse and Aoife

Please note that the maps in this book are schematic and are not intended to be a highly accurate portrayal of the topography. Orientation does not always correspond to compass points, i.e. 'up' on the maps is not necessarily equivalent to 'north'.

Acknowledgements

I would like to thank the following organisations and individuals for their support and assistance with this book: Visit Belfast, Tourism NI, Belfast City Council, Belfast Hills Partnership, Connswater Community Greenway, Fáilte Feirste Thiar (Visit West Belfast), Ulster Wildlife Trust, Walk NI, Outdoor Recreation NI, Spectrum Centre, Lagan Valley Regional Park, Sarah Nelson, Dara Barratt, Jim Edgar, Bobby Foster, Laura Kelly, Wendy Langham, Ivan Baxter, Imelda McConnell, Bobby Foster and Dan Clarke.

Picture credits

Sarah Nelson: pages 15, 18, 164, 169, 173, 176 and 178; Tourism NI: pages 17, 26, 27, 28, 31, 47, 49, 54, 97, 99, 104, 109, 115, 116, 131, 133, 141, 143, 147, 151, 156, 172, 183 and 185; Belfast Waterfront: page 26; Belfast Hills Partnership: pages 33, 38, 40, 53, 58 and 60; Bradley Quinn, Tourism NI: pages 47 and 71; Connswater Community Greenway: page 65; Paul Hunter, Connswater Community Greenway: pages 66, 83 and 84; Paul Lindsay, Connswater Community Greenway: page 75; Ulster Wildlife Trust: page 79; Fáilte Feirste Thiar (Visit West Belfast): pages 91, 122 and 125; Daniel Clarke: page 163.
Front cover photo courtesy of Shutterstock. Back cover photo courtesy of Tourism NI.

Contents

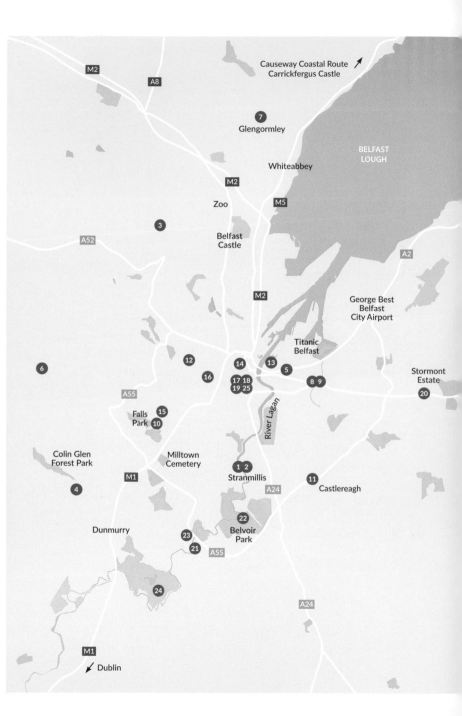

Causeway Coastal Route
Carrickfergus Castle

7 Glengormley

Whiteabbey

BELFAST LOUGH

M2

Zoo

M5

Belfast Castle

A2

M2

George Best Belfast City Airport

3

A52

6

12

Titanic Belfast

14

13

5

Stormont Estate

16

17 **18**
19 **25**

8 **9**

20

A55

Falls Park

15

10

River Lagan

Colin Glen Forest Park

Milltown Cemetery

1 **2**

Stranmillis

11 Castlereagh

A24

4

M1

22

Dunmurry

Belvoir Park

23

21

A55

24

A24

M1

Dublin

Introduction

Imagine a city where, within moments of leaving a busy dual carriageway, you can be hiking up through wooded glades and past plunging waterfalls, or following a tranquil canal towpath through endless greenery within a mile or two of the city centre.

Yes, this is Belfast I'm talking about!

In truth, that's only part of Belfast's attraction. Barely 400 years since its infancy, its history can still be absorbed as you walk around the many urban trails in this book. And that history is probably not what you expect.

Yes, you will encounter inevitable reminders of the Troubles, especially in areas where the world-famous political murals are found in abundance.

Up the Falls Road, the striking mural art will be of republican icons, like hunger striker Bobby Sands or Patrick Pearse. A few streets away in the loyalist Shankill Road, King Billy appears to be galloping away from many a gable wall.

But that's just part of the story.

How many know of Belfast's remarkable history as an industrial powerhouse, for instance? From the mid-1800s to the First World War and beyond, this city was a world-leading centre of the linen industry, shipbuilding, soft drinks, whiskey, tobacco, rope making and more.

Throughout Belfast, that history remains tangible, not least in old linen warehouses turned into offices, restaurants, apartment blocks and even libraries.

The tragedy of *Titanic*'s demise was a symbolic turning point, the start of a downward shift in Belfast's fortunes that finally hit rock bottom during the Troubles.

But today's city has undergone a renaissance. Belfast is now full of smart bars and restaurants, visitor attractions and new hotels. Thankfully, however, that hasn't diluted its natural character.

It might not yet be quite as well established on the tourist trail as other cities in the UK and Ireland, but maybe that's not such a bad thing. There's something authentic and down to earth about Belfast that adds to its appeal, and if its secrets are harder to find than, say, Dublin's, that's all the more reason to make use of this book.

An outsider myself, I was first attracted to Belfast by its people. 'Catch yourself on', 'wind your head in', 'buck eejit', 'do you think I came down the Lagan in a bubble?' – people here tend to speak their mind. But their friendliness is genuine and their occasionally dark humour is infectious.

I got to know the city gradually, often working with local historians and communities throughout Belfast on projects celebrating their particular heritage and culture: for instance, exploring the childhood inspirations of my heroes, C.S. Lewis, Van Morrison and Georgie Best, who were born with a stone's throw of each other in Belfast's eastern quarter.

Also in this part of Belfast I worked on heritage trails tracing the lives of the unsung heroes who built the giants of the sea for Harland & Wolff.

In North Belfast I discovered other, more distant, heroes and heroines:

the largely Presbyterian United Irishmen of the north, whose beliefs of liberty and equality might have saved Ireland much of the pain it has since suffered had they succeeded. Henry Joy McCracken was their leader, but perhaps even more inspirational was his sister Mary Ann, a prototype feminist and social reformer who was actively campaigning against slavery into her nineties.

Later social campaigners included the redoubtable Winifred Carney, who worked closely with James Connolly organising trade unions in Belfast, and famously entered the GPO during the Easter Rising of 1916 armed with a revolver and a typewriter.

Research for 'Belfast Bred' – a dramatised food tour I wrote for Kabosh Theatre – revealed yet another perspective of the city, not least in Belfast's answer to Dublin's Temple Bar, the Cathedral Quarter.

And then I discovered the idyllic countryside that surrounds the city and, in some instances, intrudes deep within it.

The Lagan Towpath dissects any number of delightful parks, as you follow the trail alongside canal and river. Other walks take you back to revolutionary times, offering the spectacular view from Cave Hill, where the United Irishmen swore their oath of allegiance.

I hope you enjoy this diverse selection of walks though Belfast's past and present, and the lovely rural world that envelops the city, as much as I enjoyed researching them.

1.

Lagan Towpath main walk

Few cities enjoy such an idyllic hinterland of greenery so near the centre as Belfast. Walking the Lagan Towpath, it's virtually impossible to imagine that you've just left a busy metropolis behind you or that its suburbs surround you. This is truly one of the great city–rural walks, and it's all thanks to the Lagan Navigation.

Belfast's nineteenth-century status as an industrial powerhouse could not have been achieved without the Lagan Navigation. It was one of a network of waterways running through Ireland which ensured that heavy goods could be transported much more efficiently and quickly than by road.

Work on the Lagan Navigation began in 1756 and reached Lisburn in 1763 (it was later extended to Lough Neagh). Eventually it was possible to transport goods by water from Belfast to nearly every major town and city

City Centre

NEWFORGE
LANE

A55

LAGAN
CANAL

LAGAN
CANAL

BALLYSKEAGH RD

Tullynacross
Rd

Bridge St

LEGEND

1. Car park at the bottom of Lockview Road in Stranmillis – Start
2. Belfast Boat Club
3. Lock 1
4. Entrance to Lagan Meadows
5. Lagan Meadows Nature Reserve
6. Lock 2
7. Moreland Meadows
8. Bridge
9. Belvoir Forest Park
10. Red footbridge
11. Lock Keeper's Inn & Visitor Centre/ The Industry Barge
12. John Luke Bridge
13. Clement Wilson Park
14. Barnett Demesne
15. Shaw's Bridge
16. Old stone Shaw's Bridge
17. Mary Peters Track
18. Gilchrist Bridge
19. Lock 4
20. Eel Weir
21. Malone Golf Course
22. Drum House
23. Sir Thomas and Lady Dixon Park
24. Small footbridge
25. Small green iron bridge
26. Lock 8
27. Ballyskeagh Bridge
28. Former Coca-Cola plant
29. Tullynacross Bridge
30. Hilden Mill
31. Lock 10
32. Hilden Train Station
33. Island Arts Centre
34. Lagan Valley Island/Lock 12
35. Lisburn Train Station

13

in Ireland. Where possible, the barges would follow the course of the river; where the gradient was too steep or the water too shallow they would navigate the canal.

Along the route from Stranmillis in south Belfast to Lisburn were thirteen lock-keepers' houses: a lock-keeper was responsible for operating the adjacent lock. At the height of the waterway, dozens of lighters (barges), travelling both ways, would keep him busy throughout daylight hours.

The growing impact of the railways, and later the automobile, eventually made the Lagan Navigation redundant, and when it closed in the 1950s it brought to an end a distinctive way of life. But it has not been forgotten. In recent years, much work has been done to restore this unique part of Ireland's industrial heritage, not least by enhancing the walking (and cycling) experience along its eleven-mile towpath from Stranmillis to Lisburn. The canal's historic features, such as lock houses and bridges, are now protected and much of the scenery along the way is stunning, as it dissects the Lagan Valley Regional Park, an Area of Outstanding Natural Beauty.

We begin in the car park at the bottom of Lockview Road in Stranmillis. If you're coming by bus, the 8a or 8d Metro from the city centre stops at Stranmillis College, near Lockview Road. A noticeboard at the beginning of the towpath gives you the code for the audio trail, which reveals what life was like for those who earned their living on the Lagan Navigation, and displays a map of the route. As the route begins you pass on your left Belfast Boat Club.

This was once the location of the lock-keeper's cottage. You will see on your left the restored cascade weir that once directed water along the canal. This point was the site of the first lock, named after Molly Ward, who owned a famous tavern upstream. Up to forty barges might be waiting here on a busy day, en route to Lough Neagh. Molly and her

The River Lagan winds through miles of Belfast parkland and greenery.

lock-keeper husband welcomed many canal workers to their inn, as well as United Irishmen plotting their 1798 rebellion.

This walk is simple – just a question of following the towpath along the 15.4 km to Lisburn, occasionally crossing a bridge to the other side – but there are many options to journey further into the beautiful parks you will pass on the way. From now on, it's hard to believe you're actually in a city at all.

This first stretch of towpath lies within the Lagan Meadows Nature Reserve, and there are several signed pathways to your right which will take you further into the Reserve's 120 acres of woodland and meadow, should you have time.

Look out for ample birdlife as you walk (and pay even closer attention to passing cyclists, who leave little time to warn you of their impending presence). You're likely to see herons, cormorants and kingfishers stalking fish (salmon, trout and several other varieties can be found in the Lagan).

Before the second lock (named after Micky Taylor, another early lock-keeper), of which little remains, the canal and river diverge and, should you wish for a detour, a small bridge will take you to the wooded island this creates, known as Moreland Meadows. Studded with wonderful oak and cedar trees, it's an idyllic spot for a picnic.

Another potential detour soon arrives. We continue along the towpath but you could take another footbridge on the left, which takes you to the end of Moreland Meadows, where another bridge leads to Belvoir Forest Park. This is a dedicated walk within this book, but you could take a route through the forest here, rejoining the towpath at Lock Keeper's Inn. Belvoir Park Forest is the only working forest within a city in the UK. It's renowned for its birdlife – a major reason the Royal Society for the Protection of Birds (RSPB) has its headquarters there. It also has some of the oldest trees in Ireland.

We next come to a red footbridge, which takes us to the Lock Keeper's Inn and Visitor Centre (the park rangers here are happy to offer information). Sit outside and enjoy a coffee or meal with views of the beautifully restored lock (No. 3) and the Industry Barge. The latter is a restored lighter which ceaselessly travelled the Navigation during its heyday. An onboard exhibition gives you lots of detail about the life of

From Shaw's Bridge, looking over to Lagan Meadows.

the lock-keeper and lighter operator. This is the one area on the walk where the lock, lock-keeper's cottage and stone bridge are all intact.

Just past this spot we are welcomed to Clement Wilson Park. This was developed as a public park after originally being created as a 'factory garden', landscaped by owner Robert Clement Wilson for his employees. His business was canned foods and his most famous creation was a tinned Ulster fry! We next cross over the river at John Luke Bridge and turn left with Newforge Business Park to our right. A left turn after a car park leads us back into the park. Look out for swallows, swifts and common spotted orchids here in summer.

Follow the path as it curves past a sports ground to Shaw's Bridge. Walk beneath the road and directly behind it is the old stone Shaw's Bridge over the River Lagan. Shaw's Bridge is named after a captain John Shaw who built a wooden bridge here in 1655 to enable Cromwell's army to cross the Lagan. This stone bridge was built in 1709 and was famously painted by the Belfast artist John Luke. This stretch of water is popular for canoeing and kayaking.

We won't cross the bridge but will take a gateway in the adjacent car park that leads us to Barnett Demesne. If you wish to detour to Minnowburn and the Giant's Ring (another dedicated walk in this book), cross the bridge and turn immediately right. Minnowburn enjoys wonderful views and the Giant's Ring, a Neolithic hedge monument over 4000 years old, is worth exploring.

Barnett Demesne is also one of our dedicated walks, but anyway it's worth a short detour up the hill (follow the sign) to its Georgian Malone House, a very pleasant place to stop and enjoy a meal or coffee. There is also an art gallery here.

Otherwise, continue along the towpath. A few hundred yards past Barnett Demesne a path leads to the Mary Peters Track, founded by Northern

The view from Gilchrist Bridge over the Lagan.

Ireland's famous Olympic Pentathlon gold medallist. Around the state-of-the-art athletics track are various forest and mountain bike trails if you have time for a detour.

Later we pass the modest wooden Gilchrist Bridge (1.8 km from Shaw's Bridge), worth crossing if you wish to visit Edenderry, a pleasant village very near the Giant's Ring that grew up around the linen industry and is surrounded by lovely scenery. If not, continue and you will come to some new apartments built on the site of an old water-powered linen mill. These are remarkable largely because it is such a surprise now to see buildings.

Carry on, following the course of the river on your left as it curves around, passing two more locks. At Lock 4, the canal splits from the river, forming an island. A footbridge leads to a beautifully situated picnic site where you can watch the river cascade over Eel Weir. Between the fourth and fifth locks is a peaceful stretch with an important wetland habitat for birds. In early spring and summer mute swan, dabchick, ducks and moorhen nest along the canal. Kingfishers can also be seen here, and even the occasional otter.

The river branches off at Eel Weir but the towpath continues straight ahead, following the wooded banks of the canal as it curves around Malone Golf Course. Before we reach Drumbridge, you will see on your left a huge white building, Drum House, which belonged to the Maxwell family dynasty. With a church steeple peering through the trees and the river-bank, it's easy to imagine oneself back in a lazy Victorian summer.

A little further on are the remains of Lock 6, just a couple of bollards. We now pass over a footbridge and under an old stone bridge. The signposting is confusing here. Stay on the right side of the river if you wish to continue to Sir Thomas and Lady Dixon Park (another dedicated walk in this book). Its Rose Gardens are justly famed around the world. Near the signpost is the original lock-keeper's cottage.

But we want the left side of the river. Walk around to the left-hand side and you will soon come to a little green iron bridge. Turn left and the path takes you to the three-arch Drum Bridge and St Patrick's Church, on the site of an ancient church. But we bear right, keeping the water on our right, heading towards Lisburn and Lagan Valley Island, 6.6 km away.

Some way further on, the pathway starts to circle away from the canal as the noise of the nearby M1 Motorway gets louder (though around us is nothing but greenery). We will eventually pass under the motorway to continue along the towpath. From now until the end of the walk, this is largely canal rather than river.

We pass Lock 8 and walk under the sandstone Ballyskeagh Bridge, the only road bridge designed by the Lagan Navigation's engineer, Thomas Omer. The last hanging for sheep-stealing in Ireland reputedly occurred here. Check the stonework for the grooves from the haulers' ropes.

As we continue you will eventually see on your left a very long red-brick building which for many years was used as a bottling plant by Coca-Cola. The site was originally home to the Lambeg Bleaching, Dyeing and Finishing Company, which bleached its linen here and transported the finished product by canal. This was also the site for Lock 9.

We cross over Tullynacross Road and head for Hilden. At Hilden the towpath approaches Lock 10 and crosses the road next to the old bridge. Just beyond the bridge, on your right, is the site of the most recently working mill on the Navigation, Hilden Mill. Owned by the Barbour ˹ ˑly, it was claimed to be the largest linen mill in the world and was prolific user of the canal. It closed in 2006 after over two centuries of peration. Now derelict, the vast red-brick buildings are still magnificent in their way.

Another interesting detour could be taken here, walking over the bridge and turning left at Glenmore Park, crossing Mill Street and stopping at Hilden Brewery, a family-run enterprise that offers good food as well as excellent craft beers.

As the towpath passes Lock 11, three water courses run parallel with each other: the river, canal and mill race belonging to the Hilden Mill. The towpath now runs between two housing estates. We eventually cross over to Lagan Valley Island, the site that housed the world-famous Island Spinning Company and is renowned for its links with the local linen industry. It was once known as Vitriol Island and chemicals were manufactured here from 1760. We finish at the Island Arts Centre, where there is a café and toilet facilities. Before the centre you will see the fully restored Lock 12. We finish here, but there is another 2.9 km to Union Locks, the end of the towpath, if you wish to continue.

You can now enjoy Lisburn and its history (a visit to the Irish Linen Centre and Lisburn Museum is highly recommended) or return to Belfast. It's eight stops on the train from Lisburn Station to Belfast's Great Victoria Street, or you can take the 22/22a bus from Lisburn Bus Station to Belfast (Europa) Bus Station.

Distance: 15.4 km (9.6 miles)

Average time: 3–3.5 hours

Public transport: Metro 8a or 8d from city centre (Donegall Square East) to Stranmillis College. Follow signs at roundabout for Lagan Valley Regional Park.

By car: Turn into Lockview Road from roundabout and park in the car park at the bottom of Lockview Road on the left.

2.

Lagan Towpath (Stranmillis to the Odyssey)

The Lagan Towpath walk from Stranmillis to Lisburn (Walk 1) takes you through some idyllic countryside. Taking the opposite direction, from Stranmillis into the heart of Belfast, is a very different kind of experience but just as interesting in terms of exploring Belfast's industrial and maritime heritage. The route takes you alongside the Lagan – much broader here than on the other walk – and there are plenty of fascinating detours and stopovers en route.

In recent years the Lagan has enjoyed a dramatic revival. So effective has the restoration been that seals have been seen chasing Atlantic salmon in locations like Stranmillis Weir. Anglers fish for flounder, sea trout

WALK 2

LEGEND

1. Car park – Start
2. Cutter's Wharf Bar and Restaurant
3. Queen's University Boat Club
4. Governor's Bridge
5. Lyric Theatre
6. King's Bridge
7. Botanic Gardens
8. Palm House
9. Holy Lands
10. Ormeau Bridge
11. Ormeau Park
12. Shaftesbury Community and Recreation Centre
13. Lock-keeper's House
14. McConnell's Weir
15. Cromac Lock
16. Hauler's Way
17. Central Station
18. Albert Bridge
19. The Hilton
20. Waterfront Hall
21. Belfast Barge
22. Thanksgiving Beacon
23. Queen's Bridge
24. Queen Elizabeth II Bridge
25. Lagan Lookout
26. Big Fish sculpture
27. Donegall Quay
28. Odyssey Pavilion

SYDENHAM RD

LAGANBANK RD

EAST BRIDGE ST

ORMEAU RD

RIVER LAGAN

City Centre

LAGAN TOWPATH

RIDGEWAY ST

ORMEAU RD

LOCKVIEW RD

(much bigger than brown trout) and mullet, while birdwatchers can spot the likes of oystercatchers, kingfishers and black-headed gulls.

We start off from the car park, down Lockview Road. We pass Cutter's Wharf Bar and Restaurant (with its riverside terrace) on our right and turn right after the Queen's University Boat Club to a riverside path. We stay by the river for the rest of the walk. We pass by a wharf sometimes used by the Lagan Boat Company (who provide the only water-based *Titanic* tour), then pass underneath Governor's Bridge, which connects the Stranmillis Embankment with the Annandale Embankment across the Lagan.

Further along, across the road to our left, is the wonderful Lyric Theatre, where Liam Neeson first trod the boards and is now patron. After a recent multi-million-pound restoration, it now has two theatres and a very pleasant café restaurant overlooking the river.

As we continue down Stranmillis Embankment, across the road you will see an entrance to the Botanic Gardens. This is really worth a detour, especially to see the steamy Tropical Ravine and colourful Palm House, a precursor to the one in Kew Gardens. Just by the Tropical Ravine is the Ulster Museum. All you can see from this entrance, however, is the glass frontage of the Queen's University Sports Centre. You may well be able to spot the university's rowing team on the Lagan too.

Belfast expanded rapidly in the late Victorian and Edwardian eras. When the nineteenth century opened, the population barely topped 20,000. A century later it was nearing its peak of 450,000 (it has since fallen). As the walk continues you will pass the beginning of the Holy Lands, a network of terraces developed in the 1890s which lead down to the river from Queen's University (and so house a largely student population) – so called because the developer had recently returned from the Middle East when the streets – such as Jerusalem Street, Palestine Street, Damascus Street,

Carmel Street and Cairo Street – were being named. These offer one of the most complete examples of nineteenth-century Belfast housing.

At King's Bridge, Ormeau, which divides the nationalist Lower Ormeau Road and the more unionist Upper Ormeau Road, we cross over and walk on a wide tarmacked path by the river. We have come a little over a mile at this point. The path curves around to the left, and across the broad expanse of river is Ormeau Park, the city's first, once known as 'the People's Park'. To your left are the streets of terraced houses that lead up to the Ormeau Road, also typical of the houses built in Belfast's heyday. Nearer are the artificial pitches of the Shaftesbury Community and Recreation Centre. There is a strong community spirit in this area, most obviously reflected in the Irish language centre, An Droichead, on nearby Cooke Street (worth a visit, especially when it is hosting sessions of Irish traditional music).

With the huge chimney of the old gasworks rising to our left, we come across the white lock-keeper's house overlooking the Lagan Canal, which stands at McConnell's Weir (the remains of which can be seen in the river). The keeper's role was to help the many passing lighters (narrow barges) through Cromac Lock (disused but still in existence), maintain water levels and look after the locks. In return he was given a house like this to live in, and usually a vegetable garden. You can still see the steps leading down to the river on the other side. They were used by locals, who would pay the penny to be rowed over to Ormeau Park from this side of the river. If you looked out at the river a century before, it would have been crammed with lighters, many carrying coal for the adjacent gasworks, which powered Belfast's industrial might.

The floodlights of Ormeau Park's sports pitches can be seen across the water as we press on for the heart of Belfast, passing first Hauler's Way and then Central Station. On both sides of the river are modern apartment buildings and old warehouses (fewer now than ever).

The Hilton Hotel, Belfast Waterfront, and the Belfast Barge.

As we pass the outlying platforms of Central Station to the left, look towards Albert Bridge looming ever closer. In winter up to 70,000 starlings roost beneath the bridge. If you are lucky, around dusk they will wheel up in a vast cloud – a phenomenon known as a murmuration – as they circle overhead in a truly magnificent spectacle.

When you reach the Albert Bridge you have to walk up to East Bridge Street to continue, as the walkway doesn't run underneath the bridge. Cross over East Bridge Street at the traffic lights and turn right into Laganbank Road. Follow this road around with the river on your right and the railway bridge and the Hilton looming up ahead. To your right is a small car park, once a field where farmers brought their cattle and sheep to graze before selling them at May's Meadow, a great market that stood roughly where the Hilton is now.

Across the river a large chimney is all that remains of the industry that

The Beacon of Hope, also known as the 'Thanksgiving Beacon'.

once thronged the riverbank. Take the riverside path, passing the back of the Waterfront Hall on your left. If you have time to explore it, one of Belfast's most interesting attractions is moored just along here. The Belfast Barge not only has superb exhibitions showcasing the maritime heritage of the city, but also a nice café and great views over the Lagan.

Further on you will come across the striking 'Thanksgiving Beacon' (also known as 'the Beacon of Hope' or 'Nuala with the Hula' or, worse, 'the Thing with the Ring' by locals). Standing on a globe, she is meant to inspire unity among the city's divided communities.

Walk over Queen's Bridge here by the traffic lights and then cross over Queen Elizabeth II Bridge. Across the road you will see the old ships' chandlers, Tedford's. On your right you will see the Lagan Lookout, built when the new weir was erected and the river was cleaned after decades of neglect.

The Big Fish, on Donegall Quay.

Just beyond the pedestrian bridge you will take to Titanic Quarter is the pedestrianised Donegall Quay and the colourful Big Fish sculpture of ceramic tiles, celebrating that reclaiming of the Lagan. Also here is the Lagan Boat Company, whose Titanic Tour offers visitors a unique waterside view of the Harland & Wolff shipyards. You can see more of this area in the *Titanic* and Sailortown walk.

Cross over the pedestrian footbridge and turn left and you will see the giant Odyssey Pavilion and SSE Arena. If that doesn't catch your fancy, you can follow Sydenham Road around to the Hamilton Dock. This is the beginning of Titanic Quarter and another dedicated walk.

Distance: 4.3 km (2.7 miles)
Average time: 90 minutes approx.
Public transport: Metro 8a or 8d from city centre (Donegall Square East) to Stranmillis College. Follow signs at roundabout for Lagan Valley Regional Park.
By car: Turn into Lockview Road from roundabout and park in the car park at the bottom of Lockview Road on the left.

3.

Cave Hill Country Park

Views that stretch to Scotland from 370 m (1207 feet) above sea level, links to key moments in Irish history, a chance to explore a castle and its elegant grounds – this is one of the great walks of Belfast.

However, it's not one for the fainthearted or unfit. The spectacular views come at the cost of some steep inclines getting to them. If you prefer to start at Belfast Castle, you'll find some more gentle estate trails on offer and the views from its lovely grounds are pretty impressive.

We're going for the longest walk, starting at the car park at Upper Hightown Road, around up to McArt's Fort, circling around beneath the sheer cliffs to Belfast Castle, and then around the perimeter of Cavehill Country Park back up to our starting point. It's a minimum two-hour walk, and that's without a refreshment stop at Belfast Castle.

It's not just about views. Along the way you'll encounter some important aspects of Belfast's heritage and occasional sights of interesting local flora and fauna. Watch out for bluebells, bog cotton and wild garlic in season,

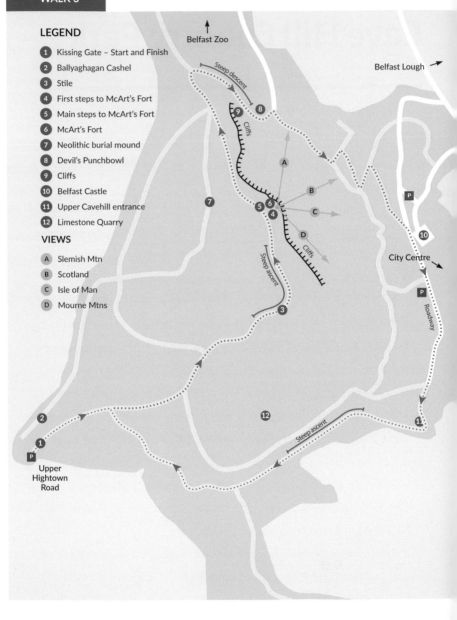

WALK 3

LEGEND

1. Kissing Gate – Start and Finish
2. Ballyaghagan Cashel
3. Stile
4. First steps to McArt's Fort
5. Main steps to McArt's Fort
6. McArt's Fort
7. Neolithic burial mound
8. Devil's Punchbowl
9. Cliffs
10. Belfast Castle
11. Upper Cavehill entrance
12. Limestone Quarry

VIEWS

A. Slemish Mtn
B. Scotland
C. Isle of Man
D. Mourne Mtns

Belfast Zoo

Belfast Lough

Steep descent

Cliffs

City Centre

Roadway

Steep ascent

Steep ascent

Upper
Hightown
Road

various butterflies, the odd Irish hare and, if you're lucky, peregrine falcons and kestrels soaring above the cliffs. You'll probably find yourself mingling with some rather docile cows too.

Walk through the 'kissing gate' (which allows people but not cattle through) by the car park and stay on the main path as you walk past fields on either side. On your left, though not visible from here, is Ballyaghagan Cashel (or Hightown Fort). Cave Hill's history of habitation goes back a long way, and there is currently some question as to just how ancient this site is. Originally thought to be an Early Christian stone fort or cashel, recent excavations have raised the possibility it may date back even further than the Bronze Age.

As you continue on the path, to your right you'll see occasional views of Belfast below, including the Waterworks and, on the horizon, the Mourne Mountains.

McArt's Fort on Cave Hill, looking over Belfast Lough.

Keep on this path, following the McArt's Fort trail and ignoring the right turn signposted for the Cave Hill Trail (you'll be coming up that path on the way back).

The first steep climb begins after you pass through another gate, where you might encounter some fairly uninterested cows as you begin the ascent to the summit. Eventually the terrain evens out and, as McArt's Fort hoves into view, you'll see Belfast Lough ahead.

There are two series of steps up to McArt's Fort and, if you're not bothered by heights, it's worth making your way to this most famous landmark from either one. As you enjoy the views across to Scotland, the Isle of Man, the Hollywood Hills and Mournes to your right, ponder on the importance of this site to Belfast's history.

You are now standing on an old ring fort or rath which takes its name from Eochaid mac Ardgail (anglicised as McArt), an eleventh-century Gaelic chieftain. It is said that the fort's inhabitants used the manmade caves built into the sheer cliff face below, from which the area gets its name, for storing food for winter. Other explanations include treasure hoards and the fruits of smuggling.

Back in 1795, United Irishmen leader Theobald Wolfe Tone met at this place with the revolutionary organisation's future Northern leader, Henry Joy McCracken, and others to swear allegiance to the cause – to rid Ireland of British rule and promote religious liberty and social equality. Three years later, after the failure of their rebellion, McCracken's sister Mary Ann scoured Cave Hill for her brother, in hiding from British troops. She found him, but so too did the British, and he was hanged near the Cornmarket in the city centre.

Known as Napoleon's Nose, Cave Hill's silhouette is said to have inspired *Gulliver's Travels*. At an angle of ninety degrees, it does look a little like a sleeping giant. Anyway, the fairly unlikely theory goes, it's what set

Jonathan Swift thinking on his regular walks from Kilroot, on the northern side of Belfast Lough, in his fruitless quest to woo his 'Varina', Jane Waring, who lived in Waring Street in Belfast.

Tear yourself away from the intimidating heights of McArt's Fort, and take the main path again. To your left a pathway will lead towards a Neolithic burial mound from 5000 years ago.

Gradually the path will circle downhill to the right with more spectacular views, including Belfast Zoo, itself perched on the slopes of Cave Hill. Further away is the distinctive funnel shape of Slemish Mountain, where St Patrick toiled as a shepherd for six years.

Continue to circle down and around, via a stile and some rather narrow steps, until you are walking towards the so-called Devil's Punchbowl, beneath the imposing cliffs from where you have recently enjoyed the views.

Even the lowest of the manmade caves at Cave Hill is not recommended for exploring.

The path becomes quite narrow, and is often muddy, and so is not recommended for the infirm or unfit. As you look to the right you will see some of the five manmade cliffs. Even the lowest of these is about two metres from the ground, and although some make the ascent to explore inside, it is not advised.

The views remain remarkable to your left until you eventually find yourself in the wooded estate of Belfast Castle. Head downwards and then right towards the castle. (It's more ex-stately home than castle but, given its commanding views, its title is not completely without merit.)

One of the most distinctive landmarks in Belfast, it is actually the third castle belonging to the Donegall dynasty. The first, built by the founder of Belfast, Sir Arthur Chichester, burned down in 1708.

The extravagant and debt-ridden third Marquess of Donegall commissioned it in the Scottish Baronial style. After his daughter Harriet sensibly married into the wealthy Shaftesbury family, the Marquess was able to complete the building in 1870.

Its greatest feature is the magnificent Italian-style Serpentine staircase which connects the reception rooms with formal gardens themed on the castle cat, to whom there are nine references in paving, sculpture and garden furniture.

In 1934 the Earl of Shaftesbury presented the castle and the 200-acre estate to the City of Belfast. Today, it's a major visitor attraction and, if you feel this walk is too long or strenuous, a good place to start your exploration of Cave Hill.

The Cave Hill Visitor Centre on the second floor is the best place to plan a trek and there are gentle walks around the estate, which includes a maze and adventure playground.

Frustratingly, the café/restaurant doesn't have any views, being in the cellar, but you could take a packed lunch to the lovely grounds and sit overlooking Belfast.

From here it's a longish and steepish way back. Turn left outside the castle and follow the road around. There are various options to get back to Upper Hightown Road Car Park. You could take the path that leads by the nineteenth-century limestone quarry, but we're following the road until it veers around to the left. On your right you will see a trail that leads through trees. Take the left turn and you will eventually find yourself at the Upper Cavehill Entrance. Turn right up a short stretch of road, and on your right you can rejoin the Cave Hill Trail.

Again, there will be some steep inclines as you wind your way up this path, with increasingly fine views of Belfast on your left. Ignore the path to the old mill on your left and keep on the main path until you come to the fork we encountered at the beginning of the walk. Turn left and head back to the car park.

Start point: Upper Hightown Road Car Park/Cave Hill Country Park entrance

Distance: 7 km (4.3 miles)

Average time: 2 hours (not including stops)

Public transport: Metro 11A from city centre (Chichester Street, outside car park at junction with Arthur Street) to Silverstream (Ballysillan Park). Walk for a mile heading north on Ballysillan Park, turning right onto Crumlin Road/A52. From there, the car park will be on your right.

By car: Park at the Upper Hightown Road Car Park at the entrance to Cave Hill Country Park, or at Belfast Castle if you want to adapt the route.

4.

Colin Glen Forest Park

Colin Glen Forest Park is a wonderful example of a community reclaiming its wilderness from what had become little more than a dumping ground. It was no small task. The Glen covers something like 200 acres of woodland and meadow on the outskirts of Belfast.

Tracing the route of the Colin River, the Forest Park leads upwards towards the Belfast Hills. There are several trails marked out here, including an engaging new one dedicated to the Gruffalo, which will delight the kids.

It's a walk through the city's history too. From the mid-nineteenth century Belfast was on its way to becoming an industrial powerhouse and a world leader in linen manufacture, with the streams and rivers flowing down from the Belfast Hills vital in helping to power many of the city's mills. The Glen was also full of bleaching greens, where the brown linen was turned white under the sun.

John McCance and his family, who owned the Colin Glen estate for generations, built flax and beetling mills along the Colin River. When we reach the Weir Bridge, you'll see the remains of the mill race where

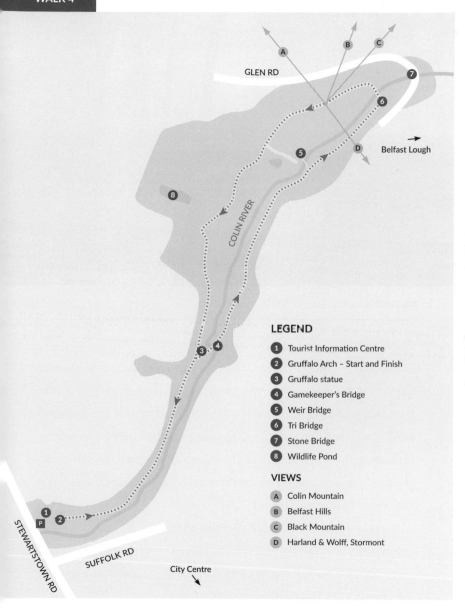

GLEN RD

7

6

A

B

C

D
Belfast Lough

5

8

COLIN RIVER

3 4

1
P

2

STEWARTSTOWN RD

SUFFOLK RD

City Centre

LEGEND

1 Tourist Information Centre
2 Gruffalo Arch – Start and Finish
3 Gruffalo statue
4 Gamekeeper's Bridge
5 Weir Bridge
6 Tri Bridge
7 Stone Bridge
8 Wildlife Pond

VIEWS

A Colin Mountain
B Belfast Hills
C Black Mountain
D Harland & Wolff, Stormont

One of the tranquil wooded walks through Colin Glen.

the water turned the nearby mill wheel.

Between the two world wars, McGladdery's Brick Works used material from the riverbed to make bricks; its pits were later used as landfill sites. By the early 1980s, Colin Glen was a disaster, full of rubbish and badly polluted. It was then that the Colin Glen Trust began its extensive restoration of the area. The river was cleaned and volunteers removed 150,000 tonnes of rubbish, while 60,000 trees were planted by local schoolchildren. Colin Glen Forest Park opened in 1993.

Begin in the car park, just off the Stewartstown Road. Take a trail map and information from the Tourist Information Centre by the car park and, over a coffee or tea at the little café there, plan your route. If you're taking kids, there's a Gruffalo gift shop to explore too.

If you don't want too strenuous a walk with the kids, stick to the Gruffalo Trail – the only one of its kind in Ireland. It's not too difficult to find, as everyone has to go under the Gruffalo Arch – 'A mouse took a stroll through the deep dark wood' – to enter the Forest Park.

All the trails continue on this path for the first kilometre or so, but we are going on the blue trail (around 4.5 km), known as the Ballycullo trail. The trails are named after townlands in the area – Ballycullo comes from the Irish for 'Corner of the Yews'.

On the walk, look out for many kinds of trees, from oak to ash and alder, along with wild flowers such as bluebell and wild garlic. As you'd imagine in this wooded oasis, birdlife is common. You might also see some red squirrels, slowly returning to the wild in greater numbers these days. As for the river, it's known for brown trout, while the very lucky might glimpse the notoriously shy otters sneaking about the riverbank.

There are some creatures you are guaranteed to see. That's because the blue trail merges with the Gruffalo Trail and along the way we meet the famous mouse and the fox, owl and snake he tricks, all modelled by Andrew McIntyre. Before we meet the main monster himself, however, we take a right fork (there are some inclines on this walk, by the way, but nothing too difficult).

The Gruffalo, in all its toothsome splendour, stands near the Gamekeeper's Bridge and there's a special themed area fenced off here overlooking the river, where you can sit on tree-trunk seats and enjoy a picnic. Gruffalo lovers can turn back here if they like.

The rest of us follow the river upwards. It's renowned for the range of fossils that are brought down each winter during floods. If you're an expert, keep a close eye, as the riverbed is claimed to be the best place in Belfast to find dinosaur fossils.

The Wildlife Pond at Colin Glen.

This is probably the most scenic part of the walk, although there will be some fine views later. The next bridge is the aforementioned Weir Bridge and mill race (aqueduct), where the water gushes down as it would have done when it was used to power machinery in the nearby linen mill at Suffolk Road.

Upwards to the Tri Bridge, so named as there are three sections to it. We will cross over the river here, but the more intrepid could instead continue up to the Glen Road Bridge, passing under the old stone bridge (taking great care) to enter into Upper Colin Glen, managed by the National Trust, and, beyond that, the Belfast Hills themselves. A long hike, but worth considering if you're a dedicated and fit walker, as the Upper Glen has much older trees than its lower cousin.

We cross the river and take the next right, passing through woodland until we reach the gravel yard on the right. Through the yard and up some steps. Take the first path on the left and cross over the meadow to enjoy panoramic views of Belfast, including Stormont and Harland & Wolff, as well as the Mourne Mountains.

After crossing the meadow you will encounter the Wildlife Pond, originally used by McGladdery's Brickworks. Around the right of the lake, now make your way back following the blue markers down to the car park, where you have earned a meal at the café.

Distance: 7.2 km (4.5 miles)
Average time: 90 minutes
Public transport: Metro 10b, 10c, 10d, 10e, 10f and 10h from city centre (Queen Street).
By car: Car park at Colin Glen Centre – entrance signposted off the Stewartstown Road.

5.

Yardmen and Narnia

We start in the heart of *Titanic* country for a walk that takes us through the heritage of those who worked on the world's most famous ship (and countless others besides). It also takes us to the childhood world of C.S. Lewis, writer of the *Narnia Chronicles*.

You can reach the start of this walk by taking the train or bus to Titanic Quarter station or parking nearby. Go through the underpass and find the path heading for the Bangor platform. Instead of going onto the platform, follow the path onto a covered footbridge leading down to Sydenham Road. Here you will be almost within touching distance of the great Harland & Wolff cranes, Samson and Goliath.

On another day you might be heading towards Titanic Belfast, Northern Ireland's biggest visitor attraction, the adjacent Harland & Wolff offices or the dock where the world's most famous ship was fitted out. But this walk isn't about the big *Titanic* attractions – more an insight into the world inhabited by those who built her.

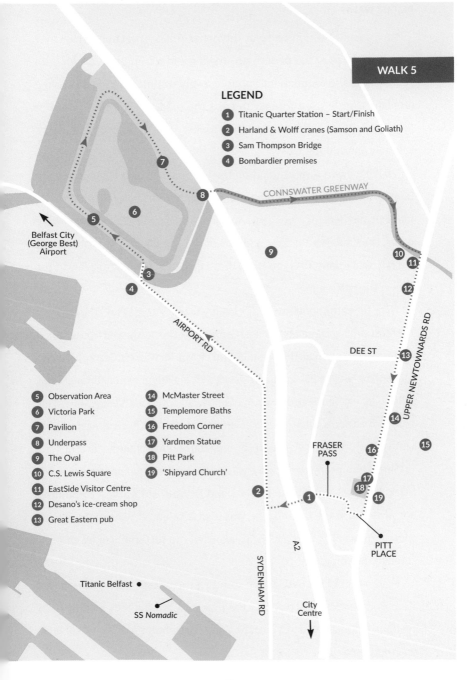

WALK 5

LEGEND

1. Titanic Quarter Station – Start/Finish
2. Harland & Wolff cranes (Samson and Goliath)
3. Sam Thompson Bridge
4. Bombardier premises

CONNSWATER GREENWAY

Belfast City
(George Best)
Airport

AIRPORT RD

DEE ST

UPPER NEWTOWNARDS RD

5. Observation Area
6. Victoria Park
7. Pavilion
8. Underpass
9. The Oval
10. C.S. Lewis Square
11. EastSide Visitor Centre
12. Desano's ice-cream shop
13. Great Eastern pub

14. McMaster Street
15. Templemore Baths
16. Freedom Corner
17. Yardmen Statue
18. Pitt Park
19. 'Shipyard Church'

FRASER
PASS

PITT
PLACE

A2

SYDENHAM RD

City
Centre

Titanic Belfast ●

SS *Nomadic*

So, instead of turning left for the major *Titanic* attractions, cross over Sydenham Road at the pedestrian crossing and turn right. Walk on until you come to the roundabout opposite a very distinctive domed building (actually a store used for salt to treat the roads in winter). Cross over to Airport Road, following the finger-post signs pointing to Belfast's Window on Wildlife.

Walking down Airport Road on the left, you will pass the premises of Bombardier on your left. Bombardier took over from Short & Harland, who made planes here for many years, including the famous Sunderland Flying Boats, the Canberra Bomber and one of the world's first vertical take-off aircraft. Walk along until you reach the main gates of Bombardier and cross over at the traffic lights.

Here, the Sam Thompson Bridge leads you into Victoria Park. The bridge is the most striking feature of the new Connswater Greenway, which has opened up East Belfast's remarkable heritage and history for walkers. Costing over £40 million, the project has gradually developed a 9 km greenway through East Belfast, following the course of the Connswater, Knock and Loop rivers. It's partly aimed at creating a greener environment for locals but is also targeted at visitors, with various trails now uncovering the heritage of the area.

Sam Thompson, by the way, was a local man who spent most of his working life as a painter in the Harland & Wolff shipyard. A committed socialist and trade unionist, he was also a talented playwright, whose most famous play, *Over the Bridge*, exposed the sectarianism he encountered in the shipyard.

Have a quick look back as you stand on the bridge and admire the art deco Bombardier HQ. Look over the river and you may see wading birds feeding. A noticeboard just past the bridge has photos of the kinds of birds you might see.

Victoria Park, where generations of shipyard workers found respite from their gruelling work, opened in 1906, the same year as Belfast City Hall. The landscaping here was created by Charles McKimm, who was also responsible for the gardens at City Hall and Belfast's Botanic Gardens. It hasn't changed much since those days. Although no longer used for this purpose, the lake here was once full of boats. The park was much loved by the yardmen and their families on Saturday afternoons (they worked Saturday mornings) and Sundays, after church.

In later years, until the shipyard effectively ended its major shipbuilding operations in the 1980s (greatly scaled down, Harland & Wolff continues in other fields, such as pioneering tidal energy projects), workers unwinding here could feel at home glancing up at those iconic giants of the Belfast skyline, the Samson and Goliath cranes, towering above the park.

Turn left after crossing the bridge and follow the finger-post to Willow Arch and then the Observation Point, where there is an information table. Now walk along the sandy path. To the left is a sea water inlet with exposed mud flats, where birds feed at low tide. On the far side of the inlet is George Best City Airport.

Eventually you will see a little pavilion, where locals start a 5 km run each Saturday morning.

The birdlife in the park is particularly plentiful in winter. Somehow, the planes landing at the nearby airport haven't affected the birds' affection for the park. The two islands in this part of the lake attract birds – greylag geese, oystercatchers, redshanks, black-headed gulls, herons, mute swans, tufted duck and grey wagtails, among many others – but the larger of the two is preferred for nesting, due to the shelter of its trees.

Continue the walk towards C.S. Lewis Square, passing a play park and bowling pavilion on your left. Here you will find the road out of the carpark that leads towards the underpass, past a small wildflower meadow. However, you may first wish to extend your exploration of Victoria Park by crossing over a bridge by the carpark to the large island in the centre of the park. It's a lovely circular walk with plentiful woodland and, usually, lots of wildlife.

Otherwise, walk along the underpass and leave the park. Turn right and follow the path to C.S. Lewis Square.

In Victorian and Edwardian times, Belfast was an industrial powerhouse that punched way above its weight in relation to its size and location – on the outskirts of Europe. And if Belfast was the powerhouse, East Belfast was its generator. Here were linen mills, engineering foundries, distilleries, the world's largest ropeworks and, of course, one of the world's greatest (though never most profitable) shipyards.

The Connswater River, which has been cleaned as part of the new greenway project, was long a key artery in this industrial success. Barges, known as lighters, laden with raw materials and goods travelled its length, and its waters powered cotton and flax mills, like Owen O'Cork Mill at Beersbridge Road.

On your way down the new greenway you'll pass Glentoran football club's ground, the famous Oval, which shipyard workers would flock to on a Saturday afternoon. Glentoran remains one of Northern Ireland's leading clubs.

Further on is the site of the Irish Distillery Company, once one of the world's largest. At its height, two million gallons of whiskey (until Prohibition in the US, Irish whiskey far outstripped Scotch whisky as the world's favourite) were produced here. The lighters brought in the barley and other raw materials to produce the whiskey, which was then dispatched the other way to he loaded onto ships in Belfast Lough and distributed around the world.

We take our break at the EastSide Visitor Centre, opened in summer 2016 as East Belfast's main visitor centre. It has a very inviting café, toilets,

Aslan looks over C.S. Lewis Square, near where the Narnia author was born.

and an exhibition with a particular focus on the three famous sons of this part of the city – C.S. Lewis, Van Morrison and Georgie Best – but which also features lots of other locals, of varying degrees of fame.

We're just around the corner from where C.S. Lewis was born. He spent the first ten years of his life in the area, later stating that 'The sound of a steamer's horn at night still conjures up my whole boyhood.'

Sculptures celebrating Lewis's 'Narnia' books by Irish artist Maurice Harron can be found in C.S. Lewis Square outside EastSide. A trail exploring Lewis's East Belfast heritage, which includes his final childhood home and the church in which he was baptised, is available from here and is highly recommended. Incidentally, EastSide is a venue for Belfast Bikes, which has some 40 docking stations throughout the city.

But we now press on, turning right outside EastSide and heading down Newtownards Road. One of the main arteries of East Belfast, it's not the most beautiful or prosperous street in the city but it has a rich history and, as you reach its lower end, you'll discover three features that reflect better than anywhere else in Belfast the lives of the people who built *Titanic* and the other great ships.

Down the road on the right-hand side, you can stop off at Desano's ice-cream shop at 344, whose homemade vanilla ice cream, made to an old Italian recipe, was George Best's favourite. It's still run by the same family who founded the shop nearly a century ago. Further down, across the road, look out for the Great Eastern pub, a listed building whose name comes from a sailing ship that operated from Belfast and whose mast is now the flagpole at Liverpool football club.

At Dee Street Post Office cross the pedestrian crossing to the other side of the road before continuing down to McMaster Street, the entrance to which is beside the Masonic Hall and opposite St Patrick's Church.

This is one of the best-preserved streets in Belfast, little changed since its nineteenth-century heyday. The street lights even resemble the old-fashioned gas lamps that would have been used here. Hardly surprising that the street has often been used for period film and television dramas.

Most of the houses were built by a developer called John McMaster to give homes to workers from the shipyards and their families. Here lived engineers, riveters, joiners, fitters, blacksmiths, boatmen, upholsterers and firemen, all of whom may have worked in the shipyard. There were no bathrooms, and washing was either in a portable tin bath in the kitchen with hot water drawn from the range or at nearby Templemore Avenue Baths, our next stop.

Turn right at the end of McMaster Street into Major Street and left into Templemore Avenue. Just up here is Templemore Baths, where you can still see the public baths where shipyard workers attempted to shift days of accumulated grime in a few inches of hot water. There are plans for a major refurbishment of the baths, which currently host a swimming pool and gym, and the original baths will be a major feature of this.

Across from Templemore Baths is the East Belfast Network Centre, formerly Templemore Avenue Public Elementary School. Many children of the yardmen would have studied here. A small exhibition retells the local history, and there is also a café and toilets.

Head back down Templemore Avenue and turn left into Newtownards Road. Cross over the pedestrian crossing here to Freedom Corner. This has long been a focus of loyalist murals, reflecting the Protestant nature of this part of East Belfast. As in other areas of Belfast, there has been discussion about re-imaging political murals with more neutral images, such as *Titanic* or *Narnia*. That has seen the replacement of many murals, but it has to be acknowledged that the original murals remain of interest to many visitors.

The Yardmen sculpture at Pitt Park with the H&W cranes, Samson and Goliath, in the background. The pink flowers are in honour of the Newtownards Road being a location of the Giro d'Italia bicycle race when it came to Northern Ireland.

Keep walking and you will come to Pitt Street Park, where Ross Wilson's statue of the yardmen stands looking across at Westbourne Presbyterian Church, still known as the 'Shipyard Church' as so many workers from Harland & Wolff attended. The sculptor imagines the men and their families going to church on the Sunday after *Titanic* sunk, offering prayers for those who died. From here you can see Samson and Goliath, the great Harland & Wolff cranes, and beyond them, Napoleon's Nose on Cave Hill.

Built of local Scrabo stone (from just outside Newtownards) and blue stone, the 'Shipyard Church' opened for worship in 1880. Its most famous minister was the Rev. William Witherow, whose fire-and-brimstone sermons put the fear of God into the toughest riveter or joiner. Yard workers and their families flocked here each Sunday from McMaster Street and other nearby streets.

Walk along Pitt Park until you come to a tarmac area at its end. A fingerpost points you towards Titanic Quarter Station. Walk through Fraser Pass, over Ballymacarrett Road and through the underpass to Titanic Quarter Station.

Distance: 3.2 km (2 miles)

Average time: 90 minutes

Public transport: Train from Great Victoria Station or Belfast Central Station to Titanic Quarter Station. Alternatively, Metro 26 from city centre (Donegall Square North) to Fraser Street Bridge/Sydenham Road.

By car: There is street parking along Sydenham Street.

You can also start and end the walk at EastSide Visitor Centre. See Van Morrison and George Best walks for details.

6.

Divis and Black Mountain

This is a walk best appreciated on a clear day. At 476 metres (1562 ft) above sea level, Divis is the highest point in the Belfast Hills and the views of the city, the lough and beyond are worth every bit of effort to reach them. Black Mountain, which adjoins it, is just as impressive. As with all these high walks, dress appropriately, with good boots and waterproof clothing, even on a seemingly good day.

The trail we are taking here is the Ridge Trail, leading from the Long Barn Café. Just past the café, there's an option to turn left along the Lough Trail which leads you past a Bronze Age homestead. The mountain is an archaeologist's dream (important digs took place here in 2017): humans lived in the area from before the Bronze Age. That history is reflected in such diverse features as prehistoric cairns and lazy beds (ridges where potatoes were grown pre-Famine). Expert eyes can make out ancient field patterns still visible on the mountainside.

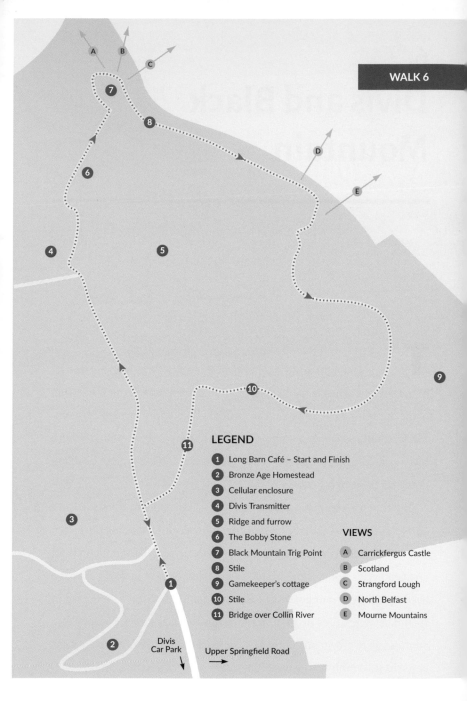

WALK 6

LEGEND

1. Long Barn Café – Start and Finish
2. Bronze Age Homestead
3. Cellular enclosure
4. Divis Transmitter
5. Ridge and furrow
6. The Bobby Stone
7. Black Mountain Trig Point
8. Stile
9. Gamekeeper's cottage
10. Stile
11. Bridge over Collin River

VIEWS

A. Carrickfergus Castle
B. Scotland
C. Strangford Lough
D. North Belfast
E. Mourne Mountains

Divis Car Park

Upper Springfield Road

A meadow pipit on the slopes of Divis.

Walking along the Ridge Trail (which shares the tarmacked road with part of the Summit Trail), we pass the walkway we will return along on the right. This is a working farm, so expect to see cattle munching away in the fields. You might also see less domestic animals, such as rabbits or even Irish hares, identified by their large ears, russet coats and size (they are much bigger than rabbits). Burnet moths, highly visible with their bright red wing spots, are also in evidence.

Birdwatchers should look out for stonechats, skylarks and ravens; you might even see a peregrine falcon or buzzard. If you're venturing out in autumn you'll encounter considerable evidence of a very distinctive wildflower, the curiously named Devil's-bit scabious, which sports a purple head and what could be taken for antlers! You'll also find different varieties of orchids.

A transmitter mast ahead high up on your left marks the area near the Divis summit in which a trigonometry pillar marks the first point used in

The H&W cranes, seen from Divis Mountain.

the mapping of Ireland in 1825. This involved measuring angles from the pillar to other trig points to achieve precise mapping details. It was a laborious, lengthy and occasionally fatal pursuit as it meant long stays on the highest peaks, often in the worst of weather.

Spare a thought for those who endured so much to ensure that our maps are accurate as you enjoy the views here.

We turn right just after the path to Divis Summit, circling around before the large masts that transmit TV, radio and digital signals to Northern Ireland. On our right we pass the famous 'Bobby Stone', actually an erratic deposit left by glaciers during the Ice Age. It was fractured by the British Army, presumably in firing practice. This entire walk would have been impossible before 2003, when the area was finally vacated by the Ministry of Defence after a presence of 50 years (hence the unspoilt nature of the flora, an ethos upheld since by the Belfast Hills Partnership).

The next point of interest is the trigonometry pillar that marks the summit of Black Mountain. Like its partner on the Divis summit, it was used in the 1825 mapping of Ireland.

And just like the summit at Divis, the views are remarkable. Weather conditions are crucial, obviously, but on a really clear sunny day you will be able to see Scotland, Strangford Lough, the Isle of Man and the Lake District in England. Binoculars will help you pick out the Anglo-Norman Carrickfergus Castle on the left (northern) side of the lough.

We continue to follow the path along the ridge, crossing a stile. As you weave around, the views change to those of the city itself: perhaps the best vantage point of all for the Belfast skyline. The Mourne Mountains of County Down frame the horizon.

Now the path circles to the right, eventually crossing another stile and over the bridge across the Collin River until you reach the main pathway and take a left turn towards the Long Barn Café and Rangers' Office.

You should be able to do this walk in a reasonable time if you don't deviate from the route, which is over gravel paths, tarmacked road, stone paving and wooden boardwalks.

Distance: 6.8 km (4.2 miles)

Average time: 2 to 2.5 hours

Public transport: Ulsterbus 106 from Belfast's Europa Bus Station to Upper Springfield Road. Walk up Divis Road to the entrance.

By car: From the M1 take the A55 (signposted Falls). Access from Divis Road, off Upper Springfield Road. Signposted from Monagh Road. There is a free car park on the other side of the road to the entrance and one further along, just by the Long Barn Café (fees apply). Check for seasonal times for the café and car parks.

7.

Carnmoney Hill

Like Colin Glen in west Belfast, Carnmoney Hill is a shining example of a local community taking ownership of its surroundings and making them accessible to all. This beautiful spot in the Newtownabbey area of Belfast, just on the edge of the large Rathcoole Estate, has been enthusiastically supported by local residents.

Working with the local council and others, they have devised a series of trails on the hill, developed a wildlife lake which attracts a large range of birds, and created a pleasant grassy area at the entrance to the walks with various sculptures.

The hill ('Carnmoney' comes from the Irish for 'cairn of the bog') has an unusual claim to fame. It was here in 1910 that Lillian Bland became the first woman to build and fly her own plane (for about quarter of a mile).

Human habitation on the hill may go back to the Bronze Age, while Dunanney Rath remains from the Early Christian Era.

You can park in the road outside Rathfern Community Centre on Knockenagh Avenue. You'll find the entrance to the walks by a gate with an

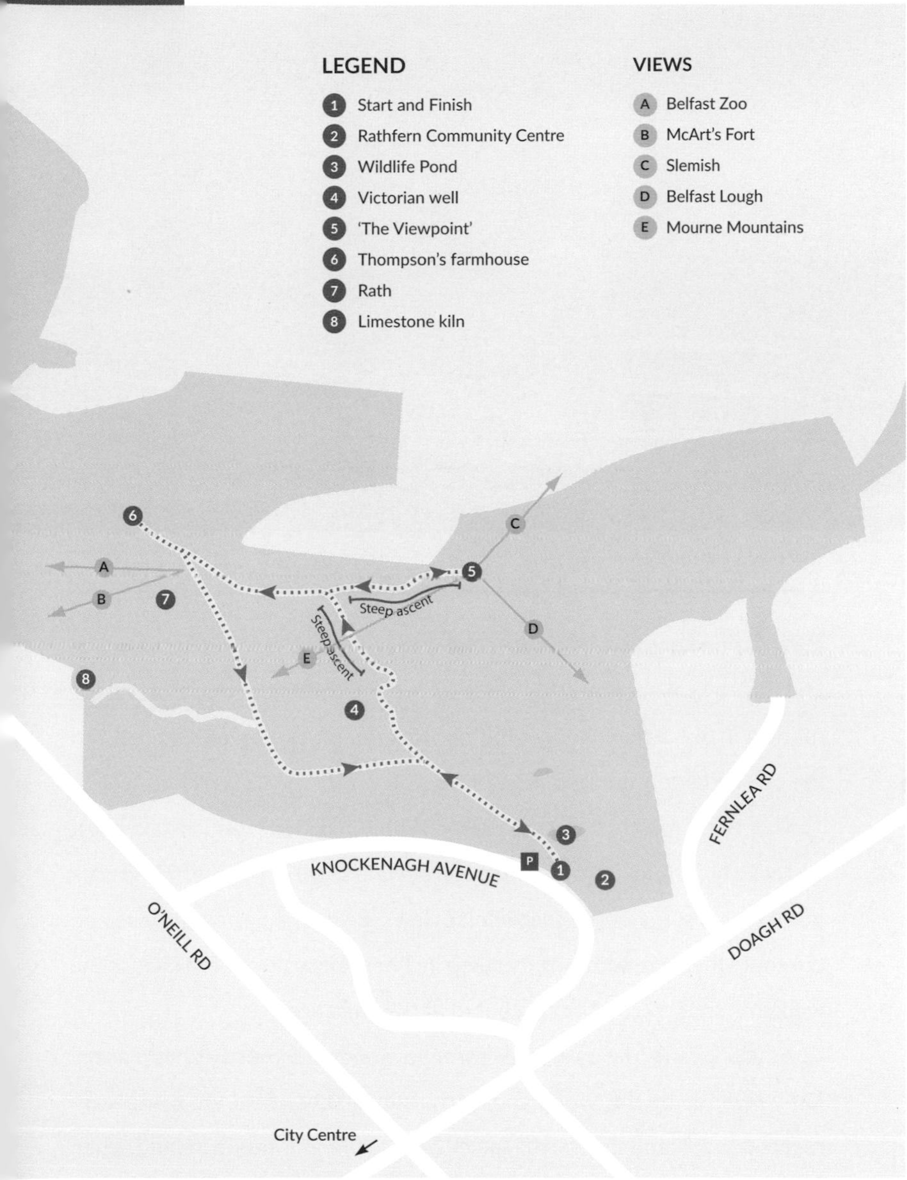

LEGEND

1 Start and Finish
2 Rathfern Community Centre
3 Wildlife Pond
4 Victorian well
5 'The Viewpoint'
6 Thompson's farmhouse
7 Rath
8 Limestone kiln

VIEWS

A Belfast Zoo
B McArt's Fort
C Slemish
D Belfast Lough
E Mourne Mountains

Steep ascent

Steep ascent

C

D

A

B

E

FERNLEA RD

KNOCKENAGH AVENUE

O'NEILL RD

DOAGH RD

City Centre

The entrance to Carnmoney Hill.

information board that describes the walks, which offer a choice of length and difficulty. A short and gentle stroll around the wooded wildlife lake is marked in red, a much longer hilltop walk (about two hours) in blue, and the one we largely follow is in yellow.

This is a circular route, the Lower Woodland Walk, which takes just under an hour. And don't worry, we will deviate slightly into the hilltop walk just to catch some of the spectacular views. Be warned, though – even on our route there are some pretty steep inclines. Anyway, you can choose the walk that suits you best from a board at the entrance.

As you ascend, the path leads through woodland: mostly trees planted fairly recently by the Woodland Trust, but further afield are some fragments of woodland that can be traced back to pre-Plantation Ireland, when the serious business of deforesting the country began.

Boards on this walk will alert you to the possibility of seeing buzzards, long-eared owls and sparrow hawks, but such sightings are not common. You probably won't see the resident badgers, foxes or Irish hares either. The flora is another matter; in season the hills really are alive with bluebells, wild garlic, primroses and purple orchids.

As we wind uphill the first site we see, on the left, is a Victorian well, recently refurbished with artwork from locals. This was once used to service the great house of the area, now no longer in existence.

We continue up the path, which is fairly steep for a while, until we reach the top of the yellow trail, where it joins the blue trail. There is a bench on the other side of the terrain as the path evens out.

If you have the energy, it's well worth turning right here and heading up the increasingly steep path, through a patch of woodland, until it opens out by an old stone wall. It's known as 'the Viewpoint', and it's easy to see why.

There are stunning views of the city right across Belfast Lough and as far as the Mournes in the south. Slemish Mountain, where St Patrick spent six years as a shepherd, lies north-east, and strictly north you are looking at the Antrim Coast. Scramble down – it is that steep – and return down the path you ascended.

Now carry on for a while, enjoying views of McArt's Fort and Belfast Zoo on Cave Hill ahead. Ignore the path to the left for now – you will turn down here on your return – and make your way to the remains of Thompson's farmhouse, probably built in the 1830s.

It's incredible to think that a farmhouse could be built in such an isolated area, but perhaps even more so to realise that a descendant of John Thompson, the original owner, lived in this dwelling until it burned down in the 1960s.

View of Cave Hill from Carnmoney Hill.

The walls of the farmhouse are still intact and there are remains of various outbuildings too. Such places would not have been uncommon in the Belfast Hills, strange as that seems to us nowadays. It's worth spending a few minutes exploring this site, reading the information board and pondering on what life must have been life for those who lived here.

You could take the path down from the other side of the farmhouse to a limestone kiln. Here limestone, quarried in the hill, was processed to create lime, a valued commodity as it was used as both a fertiliser for the fields and mortar for building. Either return up to the farmhouse or walk along the road at the bottom to go back to the centre.

We return the way we came, now turning right where indicated (yellow trail), passing a pond and wildlife meadows. Follow the trail back to the start.

For more information contact the Belfast Hills Partnership (website belfasthills.org).

Distance: 1.5 km (1 mile)
Average time: 50 minutes
Public transport: Numbers 2C/D/E/F bus and Metro 13 and 14 from the city centre (Upper Queen Street) to Doagh Road. Ask for stop nearest Knockenagh Avenue.
By car: Park in the lay-by at Knockenagh Avenue, just before Rathfern Community Centre.

8.

In the footsteps of Van the Man

East Belfast has three famous sons – C.S. Lewis, Georgie Best and Van Morrison. This walk is dedicated to the last of the three. Van Morrison is one of the world's most distinctive rock singers; his *Astral Weeks* album is considered one of the greatest ever recorded. 'Van the Man', as he is known locally, draws much of his inspiration from the area in which he grew up.

This route largely follows the Van Morrison trail devised by the Connswater Greenway; it takes you past favourite hang-outs of his youth and name-checks places from his songs. Along the way, at certain locations, you will be able to scan QR codes with your smartphone to listen to relevant extracts from the songs.

We begin at the EastSide Visitor Centre by C.S. Lewis Square, as with all three Connswater walks. The greenway runs along the Connswater river,

Belfast Hills ↑

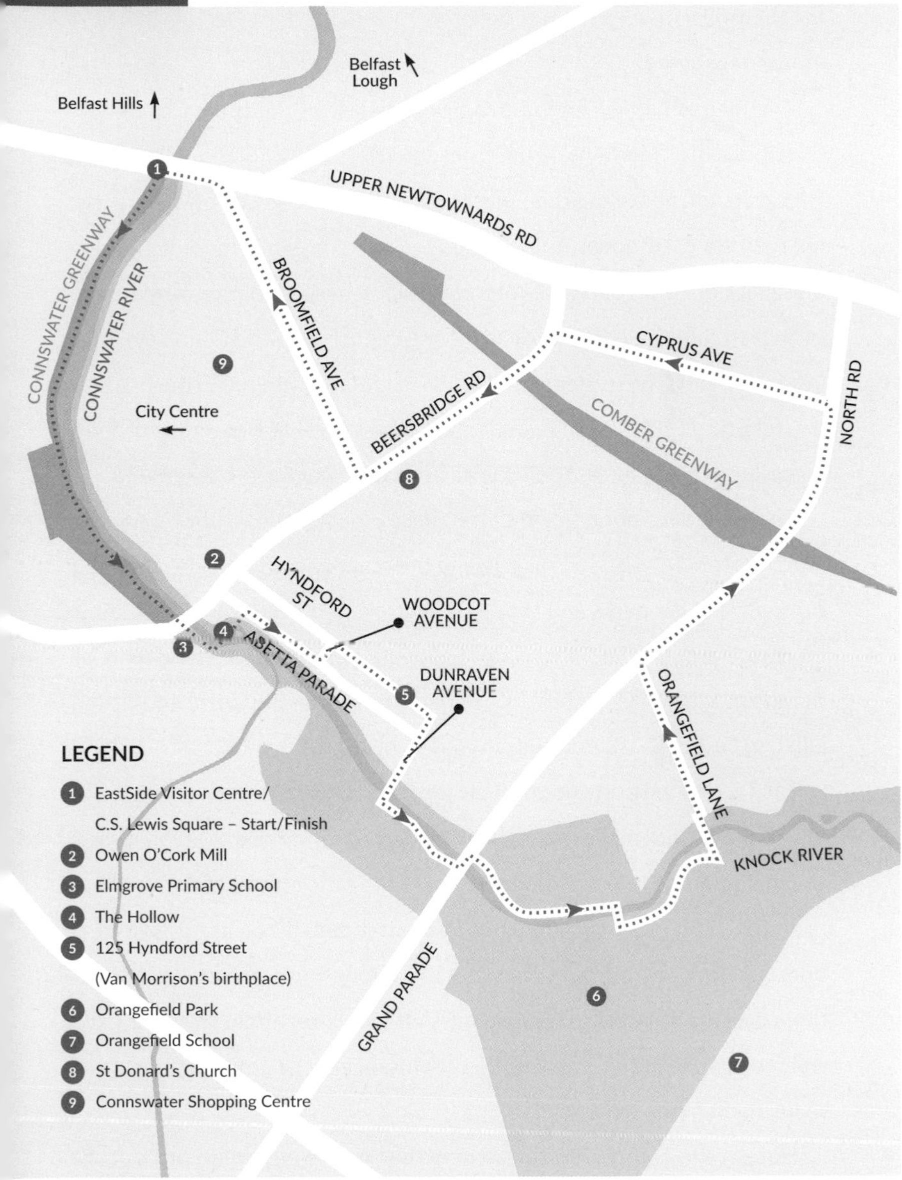

Belfast
Lough ↑

UPPER NEWTOWNARDS RD

CONNSWATER GREENWAY

CONNSWATER RIVER

BROOMFIELD AVE

CYPRUS AVE

NORTH RD

①

⑨

City Centre
←

BEERSBRIDGE RD

COMBER GREENWAY

⑧

②

HYNDFORD ST

WOODCOT AVENUE

ORANGEFIELD LANE

③ ④

ASETTA PARADE

DUNRAVEN AVENUE

⑤

KNOCK RIVER

GRAND PARADE

⑥

⑦

LEGEND

① EastSide Visitor Centre/
   C.S. Lewis Square – Start/Finish
② Owen O'Cork Mill
③ Elmgrove Primary School
④ The Hollow
⑤ 125 Hyndford Street
   (Van Morrison's birthplace)
⑥ Orangefield Park
⑦ Orangefield School
⑧ St Donard's Church
⑨ Connswater Shopping Centre

once thronged with barges (known as lighters) bringing coal and grain for the mills, distilleries and factories that made East Belfast the city's industrial engine.

The river is named for Conn O'Neill, the last of the great Clandeboye O'Neill Gaelic chieftains. Conn's headquarters were in the Castlereagh Hills, perched above the then tiny hamlet of Belfast. It was from here that his men traipsed down to Belfast one evening seeking more wine for a drunken Christmas party. On their way back, a fiery encounter with a party of English soldiers led to the death of one Englishman and Conn's eventual imprisonment. The subsequent division of his land ushered in the first successful private plantation in Ireland and the arrival of thousands of Scots Protestants. Morrison himself comes from an Ulster Scots background.

The walk does not enjoy the most auspicious of starts, but be patient. The river is narrow as you set out, and the scenery on both sides is largely composed of car parks and shopping centres for a little while. It's hard to imagine now, but the Connswater Shopping Centre across the river is on the site of the Belfast Ropeworks, once the largest in the world and closely allied to East Belfast's Harland & Wolff shipyard.

Look across the river and you'll see the Owen O'Cork Mill, which began life as a corn mill back in the 1600s and was adapted for various uses over time.

Now we come to Beersbridge Road and the official start of the Van Morrison Trail, Elmgrove Primary School. Van attended this pleasant 1930s red-brick building, still a school, from the age of four for seven years until 1956. Cross over at the pelican crossing, turn left and, after about 25 metres, you will see a gap in the old stone wall—the entrance to the greenway and, from there, the famous Hollow.

Here in this tranquil setting, where the Connswater river forms at the confluence of the Knock and Loop rivers, before heading through East

Van Morrison in the Hollow by the ancient Conn O'Neill Bridge.

Belfast to Belfast Lough, Van and his 'brown-eyed girl' spent rainy days 'down in the Hollow'. The towering electricity pylons here are also alluded to in 'You Know What They're Writing About' and 'On Hyndford Street'.

Our next stop is the house Van grew up in. From the Hollow, cross over a small carpark on your left into Abetta Parade and turn right. On reaching Woodcot Avenue turn left and then take the next right into Hyndford Street. The two-up, two-down houses you find here were typical of those lived in by Belfast's skilled workers when the late Victorian and Edwardian city was a world leader in linen, shipbuilding, tobacco and engineering, among other industries.

Walk about 50 metres on the right to No. 125, now marked by a brass plaque. It was here that George Ivan (Van) Morrison was born to George, an electrician at Harland & Wolff, and Violet, a mill worker, on 31 August 1945. Van himself briefly worked as an apprentice at the shipyard alongside George. If you've ever wondered how the great singer's musical taste evolved, this house held the secret. George's vast record collection introduced his son to the artists who would influence him for life, like Ray Charles and Solomon Burke. Here, the family gathered round on Saturday evenings to sing and play, his mother backing up on piano and harmonica.

Stand in the quiet street and imagine the young Van playing Radio Luxembourg late at night, as alluded to in 'On Hyndford Street'. Continue down Hyndford Street, take a right into Dunraven Avenue. Cross over the bridge and you're back on the Greenway. Turn left and continue walking. Cross Grand Parade at the pedestrian crossing and you will find the entrance to Orangefield Park on your left. This large oasis of greenery was a place of escape for the young Van, who could gaze out at it from the school he attended after Elmgrove, Orangefield.

Gateway to Orangefield Park, near where 'Van the Man' went to school.

Now, take the right-hand path, keeping the river to your right. Pass Collyard's Bridge and then cross the river at Avalon Bridge. Keeping the river to your left, follow the finger-post directions to Clarawood and you soon reach the Kingfisher Bridge. Before you cross over towards Orangefield Lane, glance over at the river, where you might be lucky enough to see a heron or egret, and take in the wildflower meadows on each side of the bridge.

Leaving Orangefield Park behind and climbing up Orangefield Lane, you will reach a roundabout at the junction of Grand Parade, Bloomfield Road and North Road. Turn right into North Road; almost immediately cross the road at the zebra crossing and then continue along North Road using the left-hand pavement.

Walk up to Grand Parade and turn right. Head along this road for 200 yards or so before you arrive at the bridge over the Comber Greenway. Stop here and look both ways. This was once the route of the Belfast and Co. Down Railway, and the steam trains ploughing past have been referred to in several of Van's songs.

Walk on now a little further to one of the most famous avenues in rock history, as we follow the street signs to Cyprus Avenue. This elegant tree-lined thoroughfare with its large houses is just around the corner, but a world away, from the street Van grew up in. Back in August 2015 Van Morrison returned here to play an outdoors gig, the stage backing on to the Beersbridge Road, to celebrate his seventieth birthday. In autumn, when the overhanging trees on both sides of the road create a triumphal arch of greens, golds and reds, it's not hard to see why the singer found this such a mystical spot.

Walk the length of Cyprus Avenue and now turn left at Beersbridge Road, just where the stage was set up. Along here on the left, at the junction with Bloomfield Road, make a brief stop outside St Donard's Church, where Van's parents were married on Christmas Day in 1941. You can hear its bells ringing in 'On Hyndford Street'.

Now you have a choice. Go straight back down Bloomfield Avenue to Newtownards Road (in which case look out for the mural on the left which depicts Belfast's involvement in the shipbuilding and aircraft industries) or follow the Beersbridge Road back as far as Elmgrove and then pick up the greenway again.

Distance: 3 km (1.9 miles)

Average time: 90 minutes

Public transport: Take the Metro 4a, 4b, 3a, 20, 20a, 23, 27 or 28 from the city centre (Donegall Square West) to EastSide Visitor Centre, where there is also a Belfast Bikes docking station.

By car: There is a free car park at the EastSide Visitor Centre, accessed from Holywood Road.

9.

Georgie Best and river walks

We begin the third of the Connswater Greenway walks at the EastSide Visitor Centre by C.S. Lewis Square. The greenway runs along the Connswater, Knock and Loop rivers, and on this walk we will come across all three. It's also a special walk for fans of 'the Belfast Boy', Georgie Best.

From the top floor of the EastSide Visitor Centre you can see the famous Oval, home to Glentoran football club. This has a particular relevance to Best. A big Glentoran fan, he was actually turned down by the club – one of Ireland's oldest – for being too small and weak! All was clearly forgiven later, as he played here in a friendly. They may have rejected Best but Glentoran nurtured many other great players, including Danny Blanchflower and Peter Doherty.

Belfast City Airport ↗

↖ Belfast Lough

↑ Oval

CONNSWATER GREENWAY

ORBY LINK

ORBY RD

CONNSWATER GREENWAY

GIBSON PARK AVE

MARSH-WIGGLE WAY

CASTLEREAGH RD

LADAS WAY

BURREN WAY

MOUNT MERRION AVE

CREGAGH RD

GLEN RD

A55

↓ Cregagh Glen

LEGEND

1. EastSide Visitor Centre – Start/Finish
2. Elmgrove Primary School
3. The Hollow
4. Linen Court/Linen Gardens
5. Malone Rugby Club
6. Cregagh Presbyterian Church
7. Kingspan Stadium
8. No. 16 Burren Way, George Best's birthplace

9. Cregagh playing fields
10. George Best mural
11. War memorial

12. Grand Orange Lodge of Ireland
13. William McFadzean plaque
14. Lisnasharragh Secondary School
15. Marsh-Wiggle Way entrance
16. Orangefield Park

Eastside Visitor Centre.

To begin with we are following the same route as the Van Morrison trail, the previous walk. As mentioned then, the walk doesn't start auspiciously, but it meanders into much more pleasant territory and takes us to the childhood haunts of the man even Pelé believes was the world's greatest footballer.

Walk on until you reach Elmgrove Primary School, a pleasant listed building from the 1930s, which is famous for its brickwork. Van Morrison was a pupil here for four years. It's still a school today. Cross over at the pelican crossing, turn left and, after about 25 metres, you will see a gap in the stone wall. This is the entrance to the Connswater Greenway and, just beyond it, is the tranquil Hollow, made famous in song by Van Morrison.

Walking from the Hollow towards the Castlereagh Hills, you pass on your right two small estates, Linen Court and Linen Gardens. Walk through the gate just beyond this and you will come to an information board that explores the area's heritage, including shipbuilding. Turn right here along a path beside the playing fields which leads into Orby Road.

The greenway continues along Orby Road into Orby Link and then meets Castlereagh Road. Turn left and then cross over Castlereagh Road at the nearby pedestrian crossing. This leads to another stretch of the greenway. It then turns into Ladas Way and you pass an estate called Trinity Housing. Turn right into Gibson Park Avenue (still known locally as Daddy Winker's Lane!). On your right you will see Malone Rugby Club, which has supplied several fine rugby players to the Ulster and Ireland teams, including Dennis Scott, Alfred Tedford and Blair Mayne.

Continue along the road: you will pass Cregagh Sports Club, before turning left at Cregagh Road. Walk on past the school, passing Cregagh Presbyterian Church and at the roundabout cross the zebra crossing. Turn down Mount Merrion Avenue towards Kingspan Stadium, the headquarters of Ulster Rugby. Sports lovers should consider putting time aside to visit it. Tours of the new stadium and visits to the exhibition need to be booked in advance. There is an admission fee.

Now cross over into Burren Way, stopping at No. 16 (marked with a silver plaque). When the Bests moved here to the then brand-new estate, George was just two. There are many accounts of him kicking a tennis ball to school, or keeping it up endlessly on the streets around, or kicking it with unerring accuracy at the doorknob of a local shop. The house, now available as self-catering accommodation for holidays, is furnished as it would have been when Best lived here. For more details, get a copy of the George Best Trail at the EastSide Visitor Centre.

It was from his childhood home that Best left on his final journey on 3 December 2006, when it seemed all of Belfast lined the route to

Stormont for his funeral oration. He is buried at Roselawn Cemetery, on the outskirts of East Belfast.

At the end of Burren Way you will see Cregagh playing fields, where the youthful Best was appearing as a fifteen-year-old for the Cregagh Boys Club when he was discovered by Manchester United scout Bob Bishop. You can still see the doors of the old changing rooms they used and it's not hard to visualise George's mother, Ann, handing out steaming hot cups of Oxo to the shivering teenagers at half-time.

A mural of the world's finest soccer player can be seen by turning right at the end of Burren Way into North Bank. At Trassey Close go diagonally to the left towards a children's playpark, and then take a path on the left alongside a hedge. The mural is at the end of this path behind a small development of bungalows.

Retrace your steps to North Bank and walk around to Cregagh Road. Cross over the pedestrian crossing. You could take a short detour at Somme Drive by turning left and then left again into Thiepval Avenue. Where this street meets Bapaume Avenue, a war memorial is dedicated to local men who died in the First World War. The names are revealing, for this little network of streets, including Somme Drive and Picardy Avenue, marks an all too rare example of a promise kept to soldiers. The houses here date from the 1920s and were given to veterans of the war, of whom there were many thousands in Belfast. It seems unlikely that the rare addition of bathrooms and gardens compensated for the horror of the Western Front, but 'Homes for Heroes' at least gave them some hope for the future.

If you have taken this detour, return to Cregagh Road and turn left. Walk to the nearby headquarters of the Orange Order. The order represents many people of the Protestant faith in Ulster; its members are most visible in their many marches during the summer. The building is named for

Frederick Schomberg, the general sent by King William III to lead his army in Ireland, where William's ultimate victory over James II earned him the English crown and ensured that Protestantism remained the dominant religion in Ireland.

Pop in for a tour of the Museum of Orange Heritage (there is a fee for admission) and explore the history of the order and an exhibition on the Somme. George Best's father and grandfather were both Orangemen, by the way. The museum is open Tuesday to Saturday, 9.30am to 4pm, and refreshments and toilets are available (allow an extra hour for a visit).

Just past the museum, as you go up the Cregagh Road, there is a blue and white house (now a doctor's surgery) called Rubicon at the junction with Cregagh Park. On the side wall of the house is a plaque in memory of William McFadzean, who won the Victoria Cross at Thiepval Wood on 1 July 1916, just prior to the Battle of the Somme. McFadzean threw himself over a grenade in a trench to save his comrades. This was his family house.

Again, a potential detour awaits as we reach the dual carriageway at the top of Cregagh Road. Cross the A55 and you will see the entrance to the beautiful Cregagh Glen and its ancient trees and waterfalls, then upwards to Lisnabreeny where an ancient rath and spectacular views over Belfast await. It's a good ninety minutes' detour there and back, without dallying. It's also a separate walk in this book, so we won't dwell on it here.

Otherwise, turn left along the A55, a starkly contrasting experience, and continue along here for about twenty-five minutes. As dual carriageways go, it could be a lot worse. On your left are views of the Belfast Hills and Samson and Goliath, the two great shipyard cranes. Fans of George Best can take a short detour at the sign for Lisnasharragh Secondary School, where he perfected his football skills and was made a prefect.

Marsh-wiggle Way, celebrating East Belfast's link with Narnia.

We cross Castlereagh Road and continue on. Just before Crawford's Garage and just past the next set of traffic lights (a turning for Glen Road is on your right), you will see a sign for Braniel, marking the gateway to Marsh-wiggle Way (named after a character in East Belfast author C.S. Lewis's *The Silver Chair*). Here the Connswater Greenway will take you on a pleasant journey back to the EastSide Visitor Centre, past Orangefield Park, the Knock River and the Hollow, made famous in song by that other giant of East Belfast, Van Morrison.

Distance: 6 km (3.7 miles)
Average time: 2 hours
Public transport: Take the Metro 4a, 4b, 3a, 20, 20a, 23, 27 or 28 from the city centre (Donegall Square West) to EastSide Visitor Centre, where there is also a Belfast Bikes docking station.
By car: There is a free car park at the EastSide Visitor Centre, accessed from Holywood Road.

10.

The Bog Meadows

The most unlikely nature reserve in Ireland? Look to your left as you drive into Belfast on the M1. Just past Milltown Cemetery, you'll see a lovely little oasis of the natural world, home to all kinds of birds, including meadow pipits and little grebe.

A remnant of the flood plain of the River Blackstaff, it covered a far larger area until Belfast expanded in the 1960s. Historically, the area has been used as grazing for cattle, a hunting ground by the wealthy and an arena for all kinds of sports and games by the people of the city. In the 1930s it was a popular venue for gambling games, cock fights and dog fights, while lookouts kept an eye out for the police. Legendary Belfast hard men such as Buck Alec and his sometime rivals, Silver McKee and Stormy Weather, ensured that gambling rules were adhered to.

The reserve is a triumph of local activism. It was established following a long campaign to save the meadows from development by a local group called 'Friends of The Bog Meadows'. The group went on to form a local

LEGEND

1. Start and Finish
2. St Louise's College
3. Playing fields
4. Viewing point
5. Bog Meadows Nature Reserve
6. Rise Sculpture
7. Main pond
8. Viewing point
9. Ulster Wildlife car park
10. Milltown Cemetery
11. Falls Park
12. Belfast City Cemetery

branch of the Ulster Wildlife Trust, which now owns the reserve (a winner of the 'Man and the Biosphere' award from the United Nations).

The largest piece of natural wild land in the city area, the site covers 40 acres and includes open water, ponds, ditches, wet grassland, reed beds, hedgerows and some woodland. Taken briskly, this walk could last as little as half an hour. But that would be a waste. The real point of this walk is to enjoy the wildlife, which is surprisingly populous. There are several viewpoints along the way, and on a sunny day, why not bring a collapsible chair and a picnic to add to your enjoyment?

Starting on the Falls Road, opposite the entrance to Belfast City Cemetery, continue in the direction away from the city. Turn left into Milltown Row. At the bottom of Milltown Row is the Ulster Wildlife car park, where visitors can park. There is a large information panel here with a map of the site.

Walk along by the stream until you cross over it. The path here diverts left and right; take the left-hand direction. This will lead you around the perimeter of the reserve, with several potential diversions en route.

You'll pass some willow trees on your left. To your right, where the reserve stretches all the way to the motorway, you will immediately see one of the reasons this land attracts so many wildfowl. Trees reach out from the water and the reeds growing profusely from the marshy land offer protection to many species, including grey herons, water rails, snipe and reed buntings. It's ideal for breeding and you'll see many nests in the trees. The wetland contains marsh marigold and watercress and, were you to look closely, frogs as well.

As the path circles around, you'll find the first pathway leading you to a viewing point over the water. The perimeter path continues with a row of houses behind a fence on the left-hand side. In front of you the noisy motorway looms large. As you get nearer, the top of Windsor Park stadium comes into view, as does the nearby Rise Sculpture (known locally as the Balls in the Falls) to the left and the Europa Hotel in the distance. Look back the other way and you will see the Belfast Hills rising in the distance.

The path circles around to the right, the motorway a few yards away on your left, and continues for a while. In season the hedgerow here mingles with plants like woody nightshade and dog rose. In spring and summer, you may (just) hear the sound of sedge warblers singing in the reed beds. On your right you will come across a short path to a second viewing point. Look out for little grebe, mute swans, mallard, tufted duck and moorhen in the pond.

The path again circles around to the right, away from the motorway. Now you can take a diversion to the third viewing point. This is the best view of the pond and its wooded island and wildlife. Walk over the causeway here to a raised viewing platform. Follow the path to the left (turn right to go further into the interior of the reserve) and rejoin the perimeter path. Follow this until you reach a T-junction. Turn right here and circle around with the playing fields on your right.

The main pond at Bog Meadows, with Cave Hill in the background.

You'll now pass an area of grazed meadows as you walk by with the playing fields on your right. You could take a little diversion here too, to get closer to the wildlife that inhabits the areas of grass, such as stonechat, reed bunting, chaffinch or maybe even a kestrel hovering overhead. As you circle around the playing fields to the right, you will see the outer reaches of Milltown Cemetery. Keep on this path until you reach the Ulster Wildlife car park.

A wheelchair-friendly route is available here. The total distance covered is little over a mile, but with diversions this can easily be doubled. The walk could last between thirty and ninety minutes, depending on how many diversions and stops you take.

Distance: 1.7 km (1.1 miles)
Average time: 45 minutes
Public transport: Metro 10a–f from city centre (Queen Street) or black cab from the city centre to Falls Road. The entrance to the Bog Meadows is signposted from the Falls Road.
By car: Coming from the city centre along the Falls Road, turn left into Milltown Row and park in the Ulster Wildlife Car Park.

11.

Cregagh Glen

This walk of striking contrasts begins by a busy dual carriageway, ascends along a river through wooded glades and ends at an ancient rath with panoramic views of Belfast and its surroundings.

The only problem with this delightful walk is getting to the start. Ideally you would take public transport, because parking is far from ideal. Situated roughly where Cregagh Road meets the A55 (Upper Knockbreda Road) in East Belfast, the best place to park is probably along Cregagh Road, although there are no dedicated public parking sites here. Cross over the A55 at the lights at the top of Cregagh Road and the entrance to Cregagh Glen is just to your left.

A welcome board ushers you into the Glen, and it's quite remarkable how one is soon enveloped into this beautiful natural world, even though the traffic noises continue to follow you for a while. For the first half of this walk we follow the course of the Glen River as a series of wooden bridges criss-cross it.

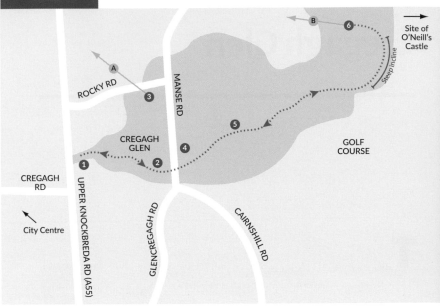

LEGEND

1 Entrance to Cregagh Glen – Start and Finish

2 Information board

3 American Military Cemetery, Garden of Remembrance

4 Lisnabreeny House

5 Lagan College

6 Lisnabreeny Rath

VIEWS

A Belfast Lough; Samson and Goliath

B Belfast Hills

Bluebells in spring, a feature of the walk through Cregagh Glen.

You walk beneath a canopy of trees – sycamore, beech, Scots pine and ash – sometimes quite dense, and with occasional plunging waterfalls it can feel a little like a rain forest, making the rapidly departing traffic noises even more incongruous. It is essentially one path so it's not hard to navigate, although there is the occasional path offwards, usually just to a viewpoint.

After a while you will reach an information board that gives you the option of temporarily leaving the Glen to visit the wartime US military cemetery nearby. If you take this option, you emerge into a large field with views of the great Samson and Goliath cranes far to your left. Follow the hedge for about 250 metres to the cemetery.

Northern Ireland was the first stopping-off point for the US Army in the Second World War as it prepared for D-Day and other offensives.

Hundreds of thousands of servicemen were stationed here from 1942.

The following year a ten-and-a-half-acre plot of land at Rocky Road was officially designated as the Lisnabreeny American Military Cemetery. Some 148 US servicemen were buried here. Most were members of the US Air Force, although they included some army and navy servicemen. Among their number were the ten airmen who perished on Cave Hill, whose story was told in Richard Attenborough's film *Closing the Ring*. A garden of remembrance was opened on the site in 2013.

Back at the information board, we now continue up the Glen, following the signs for Lisnabreeny House and Rath. This part of the walk ends as we go underneath a stone bridge and emerge into the grounds of Lisnabreeny House, now Lagan College, taking the main path ahead.

Now sensitively developed to accommodate a school, Lisnabreeny House was originally owned by the Robb family, who ran one of Belfast's

The wooden paths wind around much of beautiful Cregagh Glen.

most popular department stores. Famous for its Irish linen hall, it was known as 'Ireland's leading department store'.

It became the first property to be donated to the National Trust in Northern Ireland in 1937, when the historian and poet Nesca Robb decided that it and Cregagh Glen and Lisnabreeny Rath, all then within her grounds, should be 'preserved for the general pleasure'. To facilitate this generous gift, she actually had to help set up the National Trust in Northern Ireland, so we should be doubly grateful.

Keep on with the house on your left and you'll find yourself on a path bordered on either side by tall hedges. Continue along the path, entering a kissing gate, possibly hearing curses from the nearby but largely unseen golf course, and circle upwards around a fairly steep hill covered with gorse bushes

Keep going until you find yourself walking on a path through a field. Soon enough on your left you will see a circle of mature trees, enclosing a green mound. A wooden walkway leads you around into the green (the explanatory panel is on the far side of the rath coming from our direction, if you want to check it first).

The remains of a fortified farmstead, it is one of five surviving raths in the area, which date between the sixth and ninth centuries. Its site would have been chosen for its commanding views. Some believe it would have been possible to see the invading Vikings and Normans entering Belfast Lough from this general location.

Raths like this usually belonged to an extended family and featured several houses (wooden or clay) encircled by at least one ditch and a wooden fence. The more banks around it, the greater was the status of the owner – three could mean royalty. This more humble enclosure has just the one bank.

The settlements protected domestic animals and people against the wild animals that lived in Ireland's then extensive forests, as well as frequent cattle raiders.

Lisnabreeny is from the Irish for 'the fort of the fairy dwelling', and raths have long been associated with the little folk in Ireland. To this day there are those who swear they have heard fairy music coming from such places.

Cregagh, the 'rocky place' in Irish, dates back to medieval times, when it was part of the territory held by the Clandeboye O'Neills. Not far from the rath, near Castlereagh Presbyterian Church, was the site of the O'Neills' Grey Castle (the meaning of Castlereagh). The last of this great line of Irish chieftains, Conn O'Neill, lived here and would have appreciated its views of large parts of Counties Down and Antrim. His imprisonment in 1602 led to a division of the O'Neill lands and the instigation of the first successful private plantation of Ulster, led by Hugh Montgomery and James Hamilton, who had forced O'Neill to concede two thirds of his territory in return for his release.

We return the way we came only now it is downhill, and a walk that might take up to an hour ascending can be achieved in less than half that time returning.

Distance: 2 km (1.2 miles)

Average time: 90 minutes

Public transport: Metro 6A from city centre (Chichester Street, outside S.S. Moore's Sports Store)

By car: Turn into Cregagh Road off A55 and park along street (no dedicated public car park). A small car park is also available near the end of the route, on the Lisnabreeny Road off the Manse Road.

12.
Shankill

This walk through the Shankill area of west Belfast takes us back to the origins of the city, reminds us of its extraordinary industrial heyday and encounters numerous expressions of the area's Protestant heritage. Many scenes will be familiar from news reports of the Troubles too, while, hopefully, the Peace Wall symbolises a new era for an intriguing part of Belfast that remains largely off the tourist track.

The walk starts at the Spectrum Centre, a modern community and cultural centre at the junction of Tennent Street and the Shankill Road. With the entrance to the Spectrum Centre behind, you turn right and walk up the Shankill Road. On your left you will see the West Belfast Orange Hall, a venue for the Protestant organisation that has so heavily influenced local politics for over two centuries. Stop at the gates of the Shankill Rest Garden, about 200 yards from the Spectrum Centre.

Before becoming a rest garden in the 1960s, this area had been part of the Shankill Graveyard, the main cemetery for people of all denominations in Belfast until 1869. The Shankill gets its name from *Sean Cill*, the Gaelic for

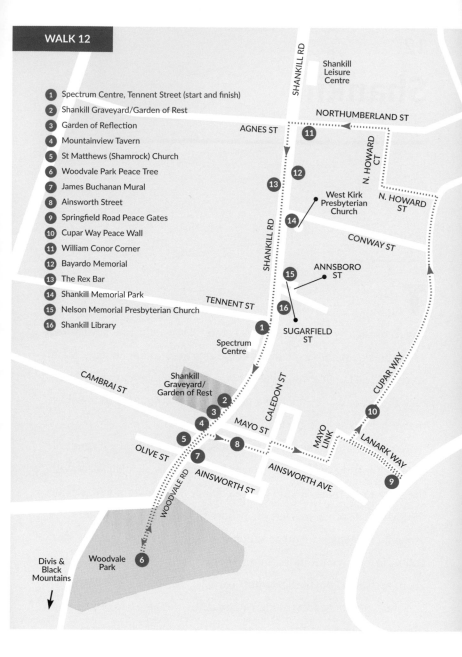

WALK 12

1. Spectrum Centre, Tennent Street (start and finish)
2. Shankill Graveyard/Garden of Rest
3. Garden of Reflection
4. Mountainview Tavern
5. St Matthews (Shamrock) Church
6. Woodvale Park Peace Tree
7. James Buchanan Mural
8. Ainsworth Street
9. Springfield Road Peace Gates
10. Cupar Way Peace Wall
11. William Conor Corner
12. Bayardo Memorial
13. The Rex Bar
14. Shankill Memorial Park
15. Nelson Memorial Presbyterian Church
16. Shankill Library

SHANKILL RD

Shankill Leisure Centre

NORTHUMBERLAND ST

AGNES ST

11

N. HOWARD CT

N. HOWARD ST

12

13

West Kirk Presbyterian Church

14

CONWAY ST

SHANKILL RD

ANNSBORO ST

15

16

SUGARFIELD ST

TENNENT ST

1

Spectrum Centre

CALEDON ST

CUPAR WAY

CAMBRAI ST

Shankill Graveyard/ Garden of Rest

2

3

4

MAYO ST

MAYO LINK

10

LANARK WAY

OLIVE ST

5

7

8

AINSWORTH ST

AINSWORTH AVE

9

WOODVALE RD

Divis & Black Mountains

Woodvale Park

6

old church, and it is believed locally (not quite so fervently by historians) that St Patrick built a church somewhere in this vicinity in the fifth century, though the first official record of a church here is in 1306.

Sadly, when the graveyard finally closed in 1958, later to reopen as the Rest Garden, many ancient headstones were lost in the transition. But there are some features of interest, including the large Portland Stone statue of Queen Victoria, carved in 1897 for her jubilee, which stands in the centre of the garden.

On the perimeter to the left a sign denotes the site of a watch hut used by armed nightwatchmen, relatives of the recently deceased on guard against body-snatchers who robbed the graves at night to take fresh bodies to surgeons for anatomical research.

Moving around the perimeter from here you'll find some interesting headstones. These include nationalist MP (very unusual for the area) the Reverend Isaac Nelson. Orange Order stalwarts mix with mariners, soldiers and industrialists and, most poignantly, many young children who died of disease in the overcrowded slums of the nineteenth century.

Turn right outside the Rest Garden and walk up the Shankill Road. Adjacent to the Shankill Graveyard is the recently developed Garden of Reflection for the 36th Ulster Division, largely composed of Protestants, including many from this area. It is essentially a memorial to the Somme, a First World War battle that became iconic for the loyalist Protestants of Ulster, as will become increasingly apparent on this tour.

We press on, passing the Mountainview Tavern on the right, known for its photos of local sporting heroes like boxer Wayne McCullough.

Crossing Cambral Street, we come to one of Ireland's most unusual churches, St Matthew's, the successor to the church of 1306 that stood in the Shankill Graveyard. Rather surprisingly, the Celtic Revival church has been constructed in the shape of a shamrock. Have a little look at the entrance door, where an ancient bullaun stone, thought to be of druidic origin, stands. It was found in the Shankill Graveyard and is thought to have been used for baptisms. A local tradition that it was used to cure warts should be taken with a pinch of salt!

When you reach Olive Street, cross over the road. At the corner of Ainsworth Street and Shankill Road stands a large mural depicting one of the many US presidents with Ulster Scots roots. James Buchanan, the fifteenth president, once said 'My Ulster blood is my most priceless heritage.' No wonder he remains popular in the area.

A further 100 yards or so up the hill is Woodvale Park, one of many green spaces created during the city's industrial heyday of the late nineteenth century for its workers. It's a pleasant little park to stroll around on a warm day, with some attractive trails, and has fine views of the Divis and Black Mountains. If you walk straight up from the entrance on Woodvale Road you will eventually come to the park's famous Peace Tree, an oak planted in 1919.

Returning towards the Spectrum Centre, we pass the intersection with Ainsworth Avenue. Take a little detour here, wandering around Ainsworth Street and Ainsworth Drive. Here are the original homes built for the many mill workers of the Shankill by the great linen magnates of the Victorian era. The size and style of the houses denote whether the residents were managers or lowly workers. See if you can judge which is which for yourself!

From Caledon Street, turn right into Mayo Street and then left into Mayo Link and right into Lanark Way. Continue down to the Springfield Road

Opposite: Woodvale Park, home to the famous Peace Tree.

peace gates, in effect a gap in the world's oldest peace wall, which separates the Protestant Shankill area of west Belfast from the Catholic Falls. Open until 9pm each evening, the gates are one of the most photographed sights in Northern Ireland.

Now we're going to retrace our footsteps slightly until we reach another famous landmark of the Troubles. Two hundred yards down Lanark Way, turn right into Cupar Way, where a large stretch of the peace wall has been cannibalised as a 'wall of art'. This eight-metre-high concrete barrier has been divided into sections, with specially commissioned murals of famous locals mixing with the work of graffiti artists from around the world. Hundreds of thousands of visitors (allegedly including Bill Clinton, though no one can find his signature) have signed the wall. You can do so yourself in the dedicated sections. The last person to step through the one gateway in the wall, by the way, was the Dalai Lama. Bizarre as it might seem, this is now one of the most visited landmarks in the city, with black cabs and tour buses regularly stopping.

Turn left into North Howard Street and right into North Howard Court before another left into Northumberland Street. A short stroll takes you past the Shankill Leisure Centre to the corner of the Shankill Road. There you will find William Conor Corner, dedicated to the local artist who won fame for his sympathetic portrayals of the city's working class.

As we turn left back up the Shankill Road, you'll be encountering many of the famous murals of the area, which are too numerous to mention. The subject matter ranges from the Battle of the Somme – in which huge Protestant losses on the first two days made it an icon of Protestant loyalty to the Crown – to loyalist paramilitary groups and the Queen.

Continue walking up the Shankill Road. On the left you'll see the do Memorial, where a garden of hope and remembrance has been set up to commemorate the victims of the blowing up of the Bayardo Bar during the Troubles. Soon after, on the other side of the road, you'll see the Rex Bar, the oldest and most famous pub in the area. The beer garden at the side features more tributes to soldiers of the First World War. If you pop in for a drink, enquire about the resident ghost.

Walk further up the Shankill Road, just past the rather grim West Kirk Presbyterian Church and you'll come to the Shankill Memorial Park. Here is a sunken terraced garden which is dedicated to people from the area who have lost their lives in conflict. A street lamp here commemorates the devastating 1993 Shankill bomb, one of the last of the Troubles. The site of the bombing is just across the road.

At Sugarfield Street, turn left and walk a few yards to Annsboro Street, where you'll see the impressive nineteenth-century Nelson Memorial Presbyterian Church, built in memory of the Reverend Isaac Nelson, whose headstone can be seen in the Shankill graveyard. His nationalist stance would not have been popular in these parts, but perhaps his campaign for land reform would have found more support locally.

Returning to the Shankill Road, walk past the Shankill Library and across the road is your starting and finishing point, the Spectrum Centre.

Distance: 3.2 km (2 miles)
Average time: 90 minutes
Public transport: Metro 11a–d, from city centre (Chichester Street, outside car park at junction with Arthur Street).
By car: From city centre, turn off Carrick Hill into Shankill Road. Turn right at Tennent Street and park near Spectrum Centre.

13.
Titanic Quarter

This walk takes you through the history of Belfast's most prestigious company and its most famous ship, right from the foundation of Harland & Wolff to its current location. En route, you'll encounter *Titanic*'s restored tender ship, the drawing offices where she was created and the dry dock where she was fitted out, plus the world's largest *Titanic* attraction. There's also a restored naval ship to inspect, and the studios where *Game of Thrones* is filmed.

Essentially, this walk takes us through the history of Queen's Island, created in the 1840s with reclaimed land from the deepening of the main channel into Belfast Harbour. Initially it was famous for 'the People's Park', which contained a zoo and botanical gardens. But after the establishment of Harland & Wolff in 1861, Queen's Island became the base of one of the world's greatest shipbuilding industries.

Fast forward to 1989, when Harland & Wolff was sold to Fred Olsen and began to specialise in marine engineering and renewable energies. As it focused on the northern end of Queen's Island, there was no longer

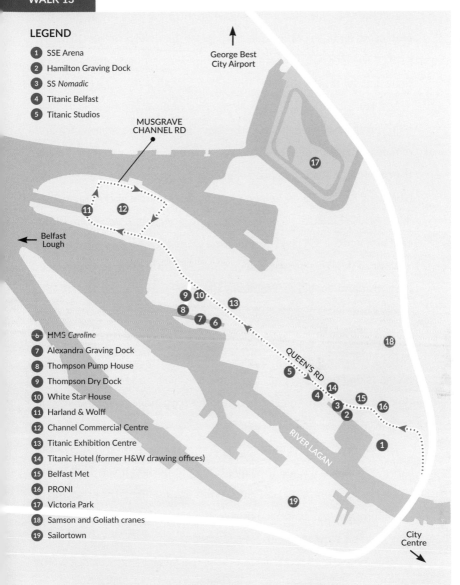

LEGEND

1. SSE Arena
2. Hamilton Graving Dock
3. SS *Nomadic*
4. Titanic Belfast
5. Titanic Studios

MUSGRAVE CHANNEL RD

George Best City Airport

Belfast Lough

6. HMS *Caroline*
7. Alexandra Graving Dock
8. Thompson Pump House
9. Thompson Dry Dock
10. White Star House
11. Harland & Wolff
12. Channel Commercial Centre
13. Titanic Exhibition Centre
14. Titanic Hotel (former H&W drawing offices)
15. Belfast Met
16. PRONI
17. Victoria Park
18. Samson and Goliath cranes
19. Sailortown

QUEEN'S RD

RIVER LAGAN

City Centre

any need for the drawing offices, dry docks or, indeed, more than a fraction of the space they had inhabited when this area was a city within a city, employing up to 30,000 people. In its place, gradually, Titanic Quarter is being developed as a combined tourism, business, community and educational hub for the city.

We start at the Odyssey Pavilion. This multi-million-pound millennium project was a vital part of Belfast's post-Troubles renaissance and remains a popular multi-attraction destination with an excellent interactive museum, W5, and tenpin bowling rink. Next door is the vast SSE Arena where the Belfast Giants, Ireland's first professional ice hockey team, play in the British Elite League. When the Giants aren't at home, the ice is covered over and the SSE plays host to some of the biggest names in music.

Walk to the junction with Queen's Road and turn left, past the Premier Inn and apartment blocks. Eventually, on your left, you will see SS *Nomadic*. *Titanic*'s little sister, the most tangible surviving link with the world's most famous ship and the last surviving White Star liner, was designed and built by the same people as the great liner. She began her life as a tender in Cherbourg, taking first-class passengers to first *Olympic* and then, on 10 April 1912, to *Titanic* itself. You can find out the remainder of her remarkable story from the onboard exhibition.

Nomadic sits in Hamilton Graving Dock, the oldest on this side of the Lagan and where she was probably fitted out herself. It was built in the 1860s, not very long after Harland & Wolff was founded. The emptying of Hamilton Dock was controlled by the adjacent pump-house, a procedure that could take up to six hours.

Walk around the back of *Nomadic* to the spectacular Titanic Belfast, which tells the story not only of *Titanic* but of Belfast's late Victorian and Edwardian heyday too. Just a hundred yards away or so, the six-storey building offers

Belfast's biggest visitor attraction, Titanic Belfast.

a ride through history and a recreation of that famous staircase and much else besides. On the way back we'll visit the hotel that stands opposite, converted from the former Harland & Wolff headquarters building.

First, walk through the vast outdoor space at the back of Titanic Belfast. Here are two sets of original slipways, one used for *Titanic*, the other for her sister *Olympic*. Two sets of illuminated blue lines show the size and location of the ships, while tall poles reveal their height. Other symbols indicate the various parts of the ships, such as first-, second- and third-class areas. Walk on to the end and you'll see the Lagan meandering into the harbour. That would have been *Titanic*'s route as she sailed out that fateful April day as people thronged the harbour.

Running down to the water at what used to be Victoria Wharf opposite is the Titanic Film Studios, including the old Harland & Wolff Painthall. On a busy day the back of these buildings can be packed with catering buses and all kinds of equipment.

You can take a short cut across the tarmac here to rejoin Queen's Road. We now pass the entrance to the tightly guarded film studios. Among the largest in Europe, it is here that *Game of Thrones* is shot, while many films have been made here, including *City of Ember* (co-produced by Tom Hanks), Spike Milligan's *Puckoon* with Richard Attenborough, *Killing Bono* and *The Lost City of Z*, starring Robert Pattinson and Charlie Hunnam.

Not far along Queen's Road we take the first left towards the old Alexandra Graving Dock. Thanks to the introduction of steel hulls, Harland & Wolff found themselves at the forefront of the trend towards larger and larger ships. Hamilton Dock couldn't cope any longer, so Alexandra Graving Dock was opened, by Princess Alexandra, in 1889.

Today, the dock is occupied by HMS *Caroline*, believed to be the only surviving ship of the Battle of Jutland in 1916. She arrived here eight years later and was converted for use as the headquarters of the Royal Navy Reserve. Recently restored as a visitor attraction, she is a fascinating ship to explore. There's an excellent film about her battle days, and the cabins have been recreated as if the crew were still onboard. The Mess Deck Café has an interesting menu too.

Incidentally, *Caroline* is half the size of *Titanic*. It's a bit of a surprise to realise that the 'giant of the sea', as the superliner was known, would be dwarfed by today's cruise ships.

Nevertheless, *Olympic*, *Titanic* and *Britannic* were far too big for Alexandra Dock. Take the cobblestoned path on the right-hand side of *Caroline*, next to the Catalyst Inc building, and you'll soon come to the far larger Thompson Dry Dock, built specially for the three ships, which were the vision of Harland & Wolff Chairman William Pirrie.

But first, instead of taking a right to view the dry dock, walk a little further on down to the Thompson Pump House. Part of the pump house,

Titanic's Dock and Pump House. The dock here was specially built for Titanic and her sister ships.

which emptied the vast dry dock, was built in the 1880s; it was extended for the building of the new dry dock in 1911. Its powerful pumping engines, housed deep in the building, could drain a full dock of 23 million gallons of water in 110 minutes. You'll discover the whole history from the audiovisual exhibition here. There's a pleasant and airy café here on two storeys.

Now walk to the Thompson Graving Dock itself. Eight hundred and eighty feet long, it needed 332 keel-blocks of cast iron to support the weight of the great liners it would hold. At the same time, a large outfitting wharf was constructed nearby and the surrounding water was dredged. Stories abound of workers getting their dinners from the fish floundering on the dock when the water emptied.

Here, in the dock and outfitting wharf, the ships' engines, boilers and superstructure were added and work completed on the cabins and rooms. Had *Titanic* not been delayed by repairs carried out to *Olympic* here, she probably wouldn't have struck that iceberg. It's interesting to wonder whether this area would be packed with tourists in summer if she hadn't.

From the Thompson Dry Dock, walk by White Star House and exit left into Queen's Road. Pass the series of buildings to your left, and warehouses across the road, until you reach the current location of Harland & Wolff, where a massive rig and several cranes reveal its latest incarnation in ship repairs and marine engineering. Turn right here and continue to the water, with Musgrave Scrap Wharf on your left. Turn right into Musgrave Channel Road and walk down towards the towering Harland & Wolff cranes, Samson and Goliath. To your left, over another stretch of water, are more warehouses.

Turn right into Channel Commercial Business Park and walk between the rows of warehouses until you reach Queen's Road. You are now roughly opposite the Thompson Pump House, part of which is now visible.

Turn left and walk down Queen's Road, passing the Titanic Exhibition Centre, just opposite Titanic (film) Studios. Cross over to the Titanic Hotel, in the shadow of Titanic Belfast. This building was the creative hub of the Harland & Wolff yard. Opened as a boutique hotel in 2017, the former Harland & Wolff headquarters building has been sensitively restored and is open to visitors. The two spectacular drawing offices, where the great ships were designed, are more than worth a visit. It was in Drawing Office One that Thomas Andrews and his team designed *Titanic* and her sister ships. The much-loved Andrews died as the ship went down, after helping as many people to safety as he could.

Cross back over Queen's Road at the lights and continue down Queen's Road. Opposite *Nomadic* is the flagship college of Belfast Met, whose students in their original city centre building would once have included many Harland & Wolff apprentices, including some who may have worked on *Titanic*.

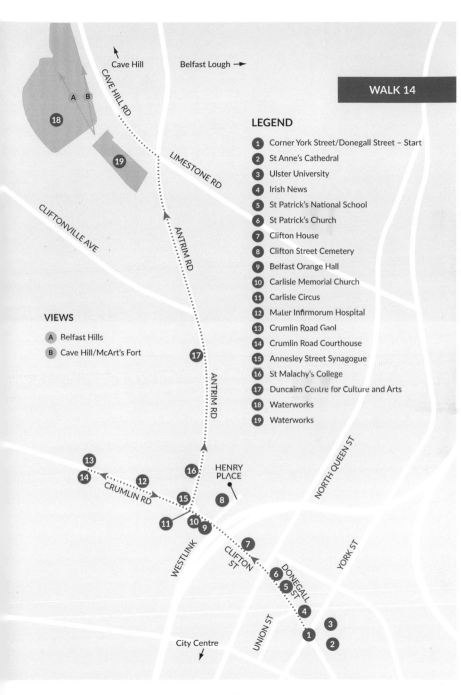

Cave Hill

Belfast Lough →

WALK 14

LEGEND

1. Corner York Street/Donegall Street – Start
2. St Anne's Cathedral
3. Ulster University
4. Irish News
5. St Patrick's National School
6. St Patrick's Church
7. Clifton House
8. Clifton Street Cemetery
9. Belfast Orange Hall
10. Carlisle Memorial Church
11. Carlisle Circus
12. Mater Infirmorum Hospital
13. Crumlin Road Gaol
14. Crumlin Road Courthouse
15. Annesley Street Synagogue
16. St Malachy's College
17. Duncairn Centre for Culture and Arts
18. Waterworks
19. Waterworks

VIEWS

A Belfast Hills
B Cave Hill/McArt's Fort

HENRY PLACE

City Centre ↙

The Ulster Orchestra playing at St Anne's Cathedral.

Union Street. Along with the gay-friendly Union Street Bar and Restaurant, located in a nineteenth-century shoe factory at the end of Union Street, it is a focus for Belfast's annual Gay Pride festival.

Staying on the right-hand side of the road, we continue up Donegall Street until we reach the first-ever Catholic school in Belfast, St Patrick's National School. The earliest surviving example of Gothic architecture in the city, it was built in 1828 on land donated by Lord Donegall. Its pupils have included the co-founder of the SDLP, Gerry Fitt, and comedian Frank Carson, who was baptised in St Patrick's Church next door. It was sensitively rebuilt following a damaging fire in 1995.

The Catholic St Patrick's Church is best known for its famous triptych of St Patrick, the Madonna and St Bridget by the society painter and war artist Sir John Lavery (who had been baptised in the church). The beautiful high altar was sculpted by James Pearse, the father of Patrick, the leader of the 1916 Easter Rising.

Like many who attended the church, Frank Carson came from an Italian background. He lived for a while in nearby Little Patrick Street, off York Street, an area so popular with the impoverished farmers who arrived in their hundreds from southern Italy in the late 1800s that it became known as 'Little Italy'. They made a lasting contribution to Belfast life, working on the marble in City Hall, Catholic churches and the tiles in bars such as the Crown Liquor Saloon. Their craftsmanship was employed on ships like *Titanic* too. Some were street musicians, while others, like the Fuscos and Morellis, left a legacy of ice cream and fish and chips enjoyed to this day around the city.

On a bright sunny day, you can enjoy the golden reflection from the brass door of the 1820 Parochial House adjacent to St Patrick's Church. A little further up Donegall Street on our right are three attractive Georgian houses more in keeping with Dublin than Belfast. These have been lovingly restored by Hearth Housing Association, a much-needed organisation dedicated to saving and enhancing Belfast's historic buildings. Sadly, others on this row were lost to road widening as recently as the 1990s.

We cross over North Queen Street at the lights and turn right, soon coming across the entrance to one of Belfast's most beautiful and important buildings, Clifton House. It was built in the early 1770s, to designs by a board member, Robert Joy, co-owner of the *Newsletter*: the longest continuously published newspaper in the English-speaking world. It belonged to the Belfast Charitable Society and became known as the 'Poor House', offering accommodation, hospital care and food to the destitute. Among those who worked tirelessly here was Mary Ann McCracken, sister of United Irishmen leader Henry Joy McCracken and niece of Robert Joy. A pioneer feminist, she actively campaigned against slavery into her nineties.

Until 1840, the Society administered Belfast's first proper water supply from here. You can wander in and enjoy the ground floor exhibition during office hours, but if you call ahead (028 9099 7022) it may be possible to arrange a tour of the whole house. Friday afternoon tours take place at 3pm, and some include a tour of the Clifton Street Cemetery.

To reach the cemetery, turn right out of Clifton House and right again until you reach the exit into Clifton Street. Cross over the Westlink at the lights and you will reach Henry Place. The cemetery is about a hundred yards down. However, it is closed to the public and visits can only be arranged by calling Clifton House or the Cemeteries and Crematorium Central Office on 028 9027 0296 beforehand.

The cemetery was set up in 1797 by the Belfast Charitable Society, which sold plots to help pay for the 'Poor House'. Here lie buried many of the great and good who made Belfast, alongside radical Presbyterians like Mary Ann and Henry Joy McCracken and William Drennan, who founded the Society of United Irishmen and gave the world the term 'Emerald Isle' to describe Ireland. Others buried here include linen entrepreneurs like the Mulholland family, who once owned the world's largest linen mill in York Street; William Ritchie, the first great Belfast shipbuilder; and the Dunvilles, owners of one of Ireland's biggest whiskey distilleries. The last burial here took place in 1984.

Across the road from Henry Place, identified by a statue of King William III on the roof, is Belfast Orange Hall. The radical, some might say utopian, vision of an independent and equal Ireland promoted by the largely Presbyterian United Irishmen of the north was virtually obliterated after the failure of the 1798 Rising. With the subsequent Act of Union between Great

Britain and Ireland, the more conservative politics of the Orange Order triumphed and sectarianism grew in Belfast. This Orange Hall was opened in 1885, its life-size bronze statue of King Billy arriving four years later.

Known as the 'Methodist Cathedral', the limestone and sandstone Carlisle Memorial Church next door now houses a Hindu temple, a striking example of North Belfast's diversity. The church is the home of the Indian Community Centre and worth a visit. Belfast's Indian community, by the way, hosts a marvellous celebration, Mela, each summer in the Botanic Gardens.

Now we come to the roundabout known as Carlisle Circus, named for a viceroy of Ireland. A statue erected to the Reverend Hugh Hanna, a firebrand preacher in the Ian Paisley mould, was erected in the Victorian era. It was blown up during the Troubles and replaced with one reflecting the local heritage of linen mills and the various faiths of the area. We are about to visit another temple of sorts, though the faith it represents is much declined locally.

Continuing up Crumlin Road we come to the Mater Infirmorum Hospital, which was established by the Sisters of Mercy. The modern building is sandwiched between two original 1883 buildings.

A little further up the Crumlin Road we come up to the Crumlin Road Gaol, a forbidding but deeply atmospheric early Victorian prison. Partly based on Pentonville Prison in London, it is built of local black basalt and sandstone from Scotland. It held a number of high-profile political prisoners including Éamon de Valera, later president of Ireland, and loyalist paramilitary Billy Wright. Since closing in 1996, it has been restored and opened to the public, and is one of the most popular visitor attractions in the city. You can explore a wing restored to its Victorian state and see the hanging cell in which seventeen people were executed.

Now we retrace our steps back along Crumlin Road to Fleetwood Street. Turn left and first right into Annesley Street and you will find a synagogue, no longer used, which dates back to the heyday of the Jewish community in the city. It was opened by Sir Otto Jaffe, Belfast's only Jewish Lord Mayor, who also established a Jewish school in Clifton Street Orange Hall and the Jaffe Public Elementary School at the corner of Cliftonville Road and Antrim Road. These were all to meet the needs of a rapidly rising Jewish population in this area, largely due to immigration from Eastern Europe. At the time of writing the unused building, which must have been magnificent in its pomp, was in a sad state of disrepair.

As we turn left into Antrim Road, try to imagine when this thoroughfare was packed with Jewish delis selling latkes, challah and other delicacies, and Lithuanian was a common tongue.

Ultimately you can take this road all the way to Belfast Castle, Cave Hill and Belfast Zoo, but we're just going as far as the Waterworks.

We now take a brisk walk up the Antrim Road. Further on, at the turning of Cranburn Street, you will see on your left, at the end of a long driveway, Belfast's premier Catholic School, the Gothic revival St Malachy's College. It stands on the site of Thomas McCabe's house, a regular meeting place of Wolfe Tone and the United Irishmen. Many famous people have studied at St Malachy's, including the man who countermanded the Easter Rising of 1916, Eoin MacNeill, novelist Brian Moore, TV presenter Eamonn Holmes and football's Martin O'Neill.

At 132 Antrim Road, Hearth has restored the lovely two-storey 1850 Woodbine Cottage, which reminds us of what this street must have looked like in its Victorian heyday.

Further along on the left is the Duncairn Centre for Culture and Arts, housed in a former Presbyterian church. Beautifully restored as a vibrant arts centre, it has a café and various exhibitions. On the other side of Antrim Road is the New Lodge area, a small republican enclave of North Belfast bordered by the Antrim Road, Duncairn Gardens, North Queen Street and Clifton Street. The proximity of Catholic and Protestant in North Belfast made it the least safe part of the city during the Troubles.

We walk up past Cliftonville Avenue, which leads to the sandstone Belfast Royal Academy, the city's oldest school. Finally we reach the Waterworks, two large ponds at different levels, which took over from Clifton House in supplying water to Belfast in the 1840s. Today it is a beautiful park, once loved by Belfast-born actor Kenneth Branagh and flautist James Galway, who grew up nearby. It became a park in 1897, when Belfast began to source its water from the Mourne Mountains instead.

Take the circular walk around the park, with its marvellous views of the Belfast Hills above. It's about a mile and a half. Begin at the Queen Mary's

The penguins are one of the most popular attractions at Belfast Zoo.

Gardens entrance on the corner of the Cavehill Road and Antrim Road. Walk up the ramp and turn right, walking past the artificial football pitch. You will pass the lower and then the upper ponds. Pass the small playground and another bridge and follow the path as it circles the upper pond. Return to the lower level and the north bank of the lower lake, where there is a multi-sports facility. Now return to Queen Mary's Gardens.

Now you can turn left up Cavehill Road, view the wonders of Cave Hill Country Park and visit Belfast Zoo, or retrace your steps along the Antrim Road.

Distance: 3.2 km (2 miles) (just to Waterworks)
Average time: 90 minutes
Public transport: 1A to 1J Metro from city centre (Upper Queen Street).
By car: From city centre drive along Carrick Hill, turn right at Little Donegall Street and use car park there (paid).

15.
Belfast City Cemetery

I t may sound strange, some might say even ghoulish, but there is no better place to get to grips with the complex history of Belfast than this surprisingly atmospheric cemetery. Here lie most of the city's most influential entrepreneurs, industrialists and inventors as well as radical social pioneers, soldiers, paupers, Orangemen and nationalists, and some of Belfast's once thriving Jewish population.

When Belfast Corporation, the predecessor of Belfast City Council, bought the land back in 1866 (it opened three years later), it was intended to be the first cemetery in town open to all religious denominations. Perhaps unnerved by this new departure, the Catholic Church decided to keep the unsanctified Protestant souls separate from Catholics in the afterlife by building a deep underground wall.

The cemetery was designed by an English surveyor and landscape gardener, William Gay, who arranged the pathways in the form of a bell.

With something like 250,000 graves, it would be an impossible task to devise an easy-to-follow trail that included most of the most historically significant ones.

WALK 15

FALLS RD

Underground Wall

LEGEND

1 Entrance from Falls Road
2 Superintendent's Gatehouse
3 Grave of Samuel Joseph Scott
4 Grave of Alexander Hogg
5 Grave of Margaret Byers
6 Drinking fountain
7 Herdman Monument
8 Gallaher Memorial
9 Mortuary Chapel
10 Grave of William Pirrie
11 Grave of Samuel Davidson
12 Poor Ground
13 Cross of Sacrifice
14 Jewish Burial Ground
15 Grave of Vere Foster

FALLS PARK

WHITEROCK RD

However, with the aid of one of the large grid maps available from the office (in the Superintendent's Gatehouse) at the Falls Road entrance (where they will answer any queries you have), you can follow this basic trail and deviate at any point that takes your fancy.

From the Falls Road entrance, we follow the main pathway. Keep straight on until you come to (about 100 yards down on your left) a monument with 'Stewart' engraved on it. Turn left here and walk down another forty yards or so until you find a very significant grave. Here lies a *Titanic* victim you seldom read about. Uncelebrated by even a headstone to mark his final resting place until recent times, Samuel Joseph Scott of East Belfast was the first of several to die building *Titanic*. A fifteen-year-old 'catchboy' carrying hot rivets to the men hammering rivets into its massive hull from the towering Arroll Gantry, he died of a fracture of the skull, probably from a fall from the gantry (grave R474).

We return to the pathway and continue. But if you wish to explore grid area S nearby you may come across the grave of a famous minstrel singer and music hall owner, Willie John Ashcroft, who commissioned the song 'MacNamara's Band' and made it famous (S125).

Although there is no trace of it above ground, the famous underground wall divides sections P and H2. Nine feet deep (the depth of a grave), its protective powers were not ultimately needed, as negotiations between the Catholic Church and Corporation broke down and Milltown across the road became the Catholic cemetery (although Catholics have been buried here for some time now).

Just beyond this point is the grave of perhaps the greatest visual chronicler of Belfast's late Victorian/Edwardian heyday, Alexander Hogg. One of the era's finest photographers, he captured everything from City Hall at the time of its opening in 1906 to the landmark Dockers' Strike of 1907 (H2).

The path now veers around to the left. At the last grave on your left before the crossroads, you will see the resting place of suffragette and pioneer of women's education, Margaret Byers, who founded what became Victoria College in 1859.

We return the way we came for a short while until we each the drinking fountain. We turn left and follow the path to the railed Gallaher Memorial, which you can see from here. In just a few yards now are the resting places of three very important entrepreneurs, representing three of the major industries of Belfast's heyday.

The first, on the left just before the memorial, is the Egyptian revivalist Herdman Monument. Alexander Herdman owned flax-spinning mills in Belfast and elsewhere, crucial to Belfast's world-leading linen industry. The steps at each side of the Gallaher Memorial can no longer be used, so the two important graves inside cannot be viewed easily (you will have another view of this memorial soon). The two in question are those of Thomas Gallaher (on the far left of the monument) and Edward Harland (on the other side).

Thomas Gallaher, an owner of plantations in the US, opened one of the world's largest tobacco factories in York Street in 1896. His company remained a Belfast institution and a world-leading industry for many decades.

Edward Harland was co-founder of arguably the world's greatest shipbuilding empire. With German-born Gustav Wolff, he formed Harland & Wolff in 1862 on Queen's Island in East Belfast and his engineering skill and business drive set up the company as one of the most pre-eminent in the world, renowned for the size, luxury and innovation of its ships.

Now with the memorial behind us we turn left, along the grassy path directly opposite the Herdman monument, and walk through until we reach the proper path, turning left. On your left at the apex of the hill is

The gravestone of Sir Edward Harland, co-founder of Harland & Wolff.

the grave of Robert McMordie. Although he was a staunch unionist and Lord Mayor of Belfast (1910 to 1914), this monument is inscribed with Celtic crosses and lettering. Indeed, around the cemetery you will see a plethora of Celtic crosses and engravings in Irish. Perhaps the most surprising lesson of this walk through history is how important their Irishness was to many northern Protestants before partition.

A few yards further on we see the Mortuary Chapel Tower on the right. It is all that survives of the original mortuary chapel, which was demolished in the 1980s after a fire.

We turn left, the mortuary tower behind us. We come quickly to a semi-circle in which a small grove contains several monuments. About forty yards after this, you will see a monument to the wife of Alexander Mayne. Behind this monument (you need to walk round to the next row to inspect it) is the surprisingly modest grave of William Pirrie, who succeeded Edward Harland as chairman of Harland & Wolff. Charismatic and tireless,

The surprisingly modest grave of Lord Pirrie, the man who commissioned *Titanic* for H&W.

it was he who had the vision for the three *Olympic*-class superliners, *Olympic*, *Titanic* and *Britannic*.

If you have time, in section K, where you are now, you will find William Savage Baird – founder of the *Belfast Telegraph*, Northern Ireland's most popular paper, which is still printed today. Another worth investigating in this area is loyalist Fred Crawford, who once concocted a plot to kidnap William Gladstone during the campaign against Home Rule. He also helped form the Ulster Volunteer Force (UVF), famously bringing in guns from Germany to Larne (including a batch he ruefully later discovered bore the Vatican crest and had been blessed by the Pope!) to arm them.

A few graves beyond the Mayne Monument, you turn left to the top of the railed Gallaher Memorial, the lower side of which we saw earlier. Here an information board reveals some of the notable people buried in the area, including Harland and Gallaher himself.

Turn around and walk back along the path, straight all the way until you eventually reach the Cross of Sacrifice. En route are some important graves including that of Daniel Dixon, another Lord Mayor of Belfast, who died in 1907, and his family. Land left by his son, Sir Thomas Dixon, and Thomas' wife to Belfast City Council is now Sir Thomas and Lady Dixon Park.

Keep going straight, past a large fountain at the crossroads. Several graves down on the left is the grave of one of the most important inventors and industrialists even of Belfast's remarkable heyday. Samuel Cleland Davidson essentially changed the world of tea drinking after his tea drying machinery, manufactured by his East Belfast-based company Sirocco, made quality tea affordable to all. He was also a pioneer in ventilation and heating and had well over 100 patents to his name at his death (D 245).

After the third turning on your right from here, you will see the grassland and trees of the Poor Ground. Remains of around 80,000 people lie in this area. Many were children, victims of the terrible fevers and diseases that spread through the city rapidly in the nineteenth century. Very few have marked graves.

You now arrive at the Cross of Sacrifice, dedicated to those who lost their lives in the two world wars. Ahead, the newer part of the cemetery extends for many acres, the Divis and Black Mountains rising up in the background. We turn right at the Cross of Sacrifice, keeping the Poor Ground on our right. The path eventually circles to the right, and on your left is the walled Jewish Burial Ground.

Belfast's Jewish population, now less than 100, was once quite large. It was linen merchant Daniel Jaffe who first requested the land for a Jewish cemetery in 1870, and it was swiftly granted. Jews began arriving, largely from Germany, in the mid-nineteenth century and there was a large influx from Russia and Eastern Europe from the 1880s. The population was focused around North Belfast's Antrim Road and briefly included a future President of Israel, Chaim Herzog. The large monument is to Daniel Jaffe, whose grave here is not marked. His son Otto became Lord Mayor of Belfast. Daniel's ghost is said to haunt this enclosure. The Jewish Burial Ground is locked (there are two gates to peer through), though you can obtain a key at the offices.

To the right of the Jewish Burial Ground is the World War I Memorial Wall. After the end of the Jewish Burial Ground and the adjacent remains of Fox Lodge, take the first pathway on the right and then the first left towards the Mortuary Chapel Tower.

Look to your left en route to the Mortuary Tower and you will come across the grave of Vere Foster (F57). Foster did more to improve the education of the poor in nineteenth-century Ireland than anyone else. He invented the famous copperplate 'National School Writing Books', which helped generations of children around the world practise their handwriting.

Now, take the path past the Mortuary Chapel Tower to the exit.

Note: The cemetery is best explored slowly. There are many graves of interest (just a few are listed here), but away from this basic trail they are hard to find. However, if you ring the office they will let you know about their guided tours. Tom Hartley, who has written a fascinating book on the cemetery, *Written in Stone*, also conducts tours during Féile an Phobail (the West Belfast Festival).

Other graves of interest include the following.

Around the corner from William Pirrie's grave, fittingly, is 'Tommie' Andrews (G182), Pirrie's nephew and the designer of *Titanic*, who perished on its maiden voyage. Much loved around the shipyard, he would probably have succeeded his uncle as chairman had he lived.

You can also discover the graves of the parents of Narnia creator C.S. Lewis. Florence (D637), whose early death had a huge impact on the young Lewis and was reflected in *The Magician's Nephew*, was a cooler, more analytical character than her emotional husband, Albert (D636). Unusually for a woman of the time, she had a first in mathematics from Queen's University.

From a Protestant background, Robert Lynd (M495) was a fervent republican and champion of the Irish language. He wrote the foreword to his friend James Connolly's *Labour in Irish History*, and spoke at Connolly's funeral.

Distance: 1.9 km (1.2 miles)
Average time: Depends how much you wish to explore.
Public transport: Metro 10a–f from city centre (Queen Street).
By car: Head up Falls Road from city centre. Entrance at junction with Whiterock Road. Parking in nearby roads.

16.
The Falls Road

On this walk you'll encounter hunger strikers, the monastery that shaped the peace process, a republican museum, an Irish language cultural centre and the world-famous International Wall, our start.

Instantly recognisable from countless television reports over many decades, the Falls Road is the epicentre of Belfast's republican community. The area has been a Catholic stronghold since the nineteenth century, yet few realise just how near it is to the equally iconic loyalist (Protestant) Shankill Road, which runs parallel just a few hundred yards away.

Our first proper stop is one of Belfast's most famous walls. Even in a city renowned for murals, the International Wall is remarkable. It stretches around the corner of the Falls Road and Northumberland Road (a short walk from the Shankill Road). The wall reflects the wider political sympathies of the republican movement and is painted by local artists. As well as murals depicting local history, sport and the Troubles, you're likely to see Nelson Mandela, Fidel Castro and anti-slavery images. Being photographed in front of these regularly changing murals has become something of a rite of passage for visitors to Belfast.

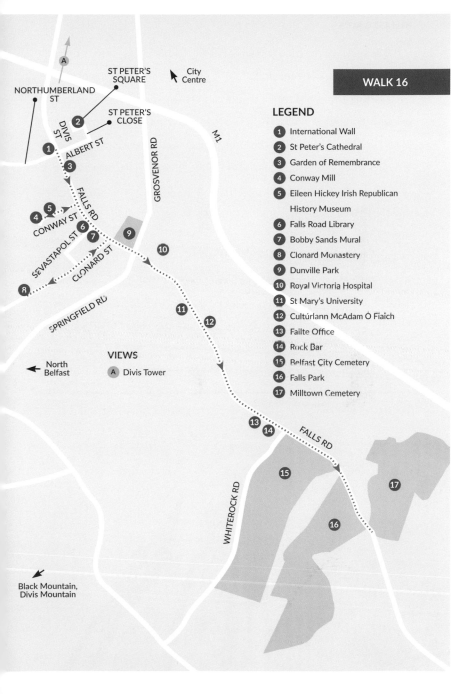

WALK 16

LEGEND

1. International Wall
2. St Peter's Cathedral
3. Garden of Remembrance
4. Conway Mill
5. Eileen Hickey Irish Republican History Museum
6. Falls Road Library
7. Bobby Sands Mural
8. Clonard Monastery
9. Dunville Park
10. Royal Victoria Hospital
11. St Mary's University
12. Cultúrlann McAdam Ó Fiaich
13. Failte Office
14. Rock Bar
15. Belfast City Cemetery
16. Falls Park
17. Milltown Cemetery

ST PETER'S SQUARE

City Centre

NORTHUMBERLAND ST

DIVIS ST

ST PETER'S CLOSE

ALBERT ST

GROSVENOR RD

M1

FALLS RD

CONWAY ST

SEVASTAPOL ST

CLONARD ST

SPRINGFIELD RD

FALLS RD

WHITEROCK RD

VIEWS

A Divis Tower

← North Belfast

↙ Black Mountain, Divis Mountain

A

Looking down the road you will see a tall tower block, famous throughout the Troubles. Divis Tower is also the meeting point for tours of the area by Coiste, a group of former republican activists and political ex-prisoners. Incidentally, as you walk up the road you'll notice a steady stream of black London taxi cabs. They became popular here in the early years of the Troubles when bus drivers, fearful of their safety, refused to drive along the road. The cabs are shared by passengers travelling up and down the road and the charge is very reasonable. It's a great way to meet the locals, so why not try one on the way back?

Cross over from the International Wall at the traffic lights and enter Albert Road. Walk down a few yards to St Peter's Close, before making your way to St Peter's Square. Here you'll find the very impressive Gothic Revival St Peter's Cathedral. Famous for its two towering spires (which unfortunately were of great help to the Luftwaffe during the terrible Belfast Blitz), it was opened in 1866 to compensate for the lack of churches for Catholics

St Peter's Cathedral.

in Belfast. The land was donated by Ireland's most successful baker, Barney Hughes, beloved for keeping his bread prices down during the Famine and inventor of an outsized floury bread roll still hugely popular in the city – Barney's bap or the Belfast bap.

Walk back to the Falls Road and turn left. You will pass the Garden of Remembrance, which lists all the republicans who died in the area from the 1920s onwards. A little further on, cross over again and turn right into Conway Street and walk down to Conway Mill.

It was the presence of several large linen mills in the area that drew Catholics in from the surrounding countryside in the nineteenth century. The work was badly paid and conditions were dire but, following the Great Famine of the 1840s, the countryside could support only a fraction of its population. Conway Mill, built in the 1840s, was the earliest of nine mills that could be found in the area by the 1860s, contributing to Belfast becoming the world's leading linen city. Unlike its competitors, Conway Mill survived into the 1970s. Sensitively restored, it is now home to a theatre, gallery and many artist workshops. It also has a café and market stalls.

Around the back you will find the Eileen Hickey Irish Republican History Museum, which offers a rather haphazard but fascinating range of artefacts, photos, articles and documents that traces the republican movement from the United Irishmen of 1798 to the modern Troubles. There's even a replica cell from Armagh Women's Prison, where ex-IRA volunteer Eileen Hickey herself spent time. Admission is free, though a donation is welcomed.

Our next stop is the famous Bobby Sands Mural. Continue up the Falls Road until you come to the Falls Road Library. Built in 1908 from funds donated by American steel magnate Andrew Carnegie, it has survived petrol bombs, explosions, burning vehicles and riots. Just across Sevastopol Street is the mural of the most iconic republican of the modern

Troubles. Bobby Sands was the first hunger striker to die (after sixty-five days) in 1981. His death, twenty-one days after being voted MP for Fermanagh West, alerted the republican movement to the advantages of electoral politics, eventually paving the way for the peace process.

Walk up the Falls Road, turn right into Clonard Street and continue up that road until you reach the first gate to Clonard Monastery on the right.

It is not an exaggeration to say that the peace process took its impetus from talks held at Clonard Monastery. It was here during the late 1980s that the leaders of the two nationalist parties, Sinn Féin and the SDLP – Gerry Adams and John Hume – met frequently to prepare the ground for wider talks. Clonard Monastery has been home to a Redemptorist religious community since 1896. The adjacent French Gothic church has a magnificent rose window over the entrance portals. Pilgrims come to this beautiful church and the grounds from all over Ireland each June for the annual nine-day novena.

Walk back to the Falls Road and turn right. At the Springfield Road/ Grosvenor Road junction use the lights to cross over to the left-hand side of the Falls Road. Here is Dunville Park, named after its whiskey-distilling benefactor, who donated it to the people of the city in 1887. Located within the park is the famous Dunville Fountain. How did he get this money? At this time, 60% of Irish whiskey (the most popular in the world until the US Prohibition) was exported through Belfast and Dunville's VR was acknowledged as one of the finest.

Cross over Grosvenor Road and past the Royal Victoria Hospital. The faces in the railings as you walk past represent past patients. The sprawling grounds of the hospital still house one of the world's first air-conditioning ducts, designed by Sirocco of East Belfast, whose tea-drying machinery helped change the world's tea-drinking habits (making Indian tea more popular than Chinese).

It is also where Frank Pantridge developed the first mobile defibrillator unit, leading to the world's first mobile coronary care unit.

Continue along on the left, past St Mary's University on the other side of the road (a regular venue for talks during the annual West Belfast Festival, of which more later) until you reach Cultúrlann McAdam Ó Fiaich on the left shortly after the turn for Broadway.

Converted from an old Presbyterian Church and named after two great champions of the Irish language, the late Cardinal Tomás Ó Fiaich and Robert Shipboy McAdam, a Presbyterian businessman, it has become the

---

Cultúrlann McAdam Ó Fiaich, the cultural hub of West Belfast.

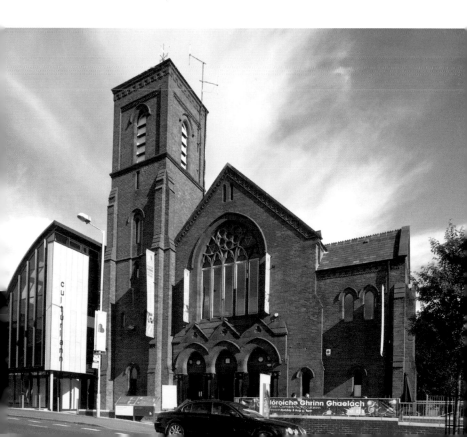

cultural centre of what is now known as the Gaeltacht Quarter. As well as a café restaurant, there's a shop selling Irish-language books and souvenirs and a gallery named after local artist Gerard Dillon. There's also regular theatre, Irish dance and music. It is a useful tourist information point for visiting west Belfast too.

Our next stop is really just a plaque, but it's to James Connolly – the Irish revolutionary and socialist thinker who was one of the leaders of the 1916 Easter Rising – and worth a visit. En route – it's about ten minutes from Cultúrlann – you'll pass the James Connolly Visitor Centre, celebrating the influential trade union leader's association with Belfast, on the left. A little further up, across the road is the Féile an Phobail building. This is the office of the West Belfast Festival, one of the largest of its kind in Europe. If you have an interest in the politics of Northern Ireland, this is the best time to visit the area, with a chance to mingle with the local community. It's usually held in late July or early August and mixes political and literary debates with exhibitions, tours, live music, film, parades and local community events.

A little further on the right-hand side of the road is the distinctive Rock Bar, on the corner of Rockmore Road and the Falls Road. It was built in 1900, around the same time as Belfast City Hall. Taking advantage of a strike by stonemasons at City Hall, the owner Frank O'Neill enlisted their services to create the pub's impressive sandstone façade. It is even said that some of the sandstone intended for City Hall ended up adorning the Rock.

Just after the mini-roundabout you'll come to 420 Falls Road, once home to James Connolly, who lived here from 1911. How long he remained in Belfast seems to be a matter of debate, but certainly he was here in 1913 to lead the textile workers' strike. As Belfast Secretary of the Irish Transport and General Workers' Union, he supported the dockers and the largely female mill workers. The plaque was unveiled in 1968 by his son Roddy.

From here you could walk over the zebra crossing to the Belfast City Cemetery. Wonderfully atmospheric and surprisingly scenic, it is a great way to uncover the often surprising history of the city. However, it is the subject of another walk in this book, so we won't go into more detail here.

Another subject of a walk is the Bog Meadows, just five minutes' walk away from here. Continue until you reach Milltown Row and turn left. Otherwise, head on up the Falls Road, passing first the City Cemetery on the other side and then the Falls Park. Eventually you will reach the entrance gates to Milltown Cemetery.

Most visitors come here to see the famous republican plot, but there is a longer history to the place. Opened in 1869, Milltown Cemetery became the main Catholic cemetery in Belfast. It is believed that approximately 60,000 to 80,000 people are buried in paupers' graves as a result of hunger and fever.

One of the most remarkable people to be buried here is Winifred Carney, suffragette and personal secretary to James Connolly, who had a great influence in establishing trade unionism in Belfast and beyond. She famously entered the GPO during the Easter Rising armed with a Webley revolver and a typewriter on which she would type the wounded Connolly's final orders. Typically, she refused to leave him, staying until the end.

Her marriage to Orangeman and Somme veteran George McBride caused dissension among Catholics and Protestants alike, which resulted in them being buried apart, Winifred in an unmarked grave. Fortunately, the National Graves Association has now erected a headstone at her grave.

To reach the famous republican plot, walk through the entrance gates and continue on the path around the semicircle until it straightens again. Then continue walking until you reach a T-junction. Turn right and walk down this path to the end. You will see the republican plot on your right.

A number of prominent republicans from recent times are buried here, including Bobby Sands, Joe McDonnell and Kieran Doherty, who died on hunger strike in the H-Blocks in 1981. Others buried close to them are Mairead Farrell, Dan McCann and Seán Savage, who were killed by the SAS in Gibraltar in March 1988. At their funeral ten days later, Michael Stone, a loyalist, threw grenades and fired shots at the mourners within the cemetery grounds, killing three and wounding numerous others.

Retrace your steps to the Falls Road and hail a black cab to take you back to the city centre. Enjoy the company!

Distance: 4 km (2.5 miles)

Average time: 90 minutes

Public transport: Metro 10a–f from city centre (Queen Street).

By car: Drive up Falls Road from city centre. There are car parking places available across Northumberland Road from the International Wall.

17.

Titanic **and Sailortown**

This is a walk with a distinctively nautical theme, tracing not just Belfast's abiding *Titanic* connections but its fascinating maritime heritage too.

We start at City Hall, which was referred to as the 'Stone Titanic' by Lord Pirrie, the Chairman of Harland & Wolff, who conceived the superliner RMS *Titanic* and her sister ships *Olympic* and *Britannic*. Pirrie, Lord Mayor of Belfast between 1896 and 1998, was also credited with having 'the big ideas' for the magnificent City Hall. Thanks to him, craftsmen who worked on the Lord Mayor's suite in City Hall, which is known as the Titanic Room, went on to build the staterooms of *Titanic*. Note its porthole windows and beautiful mahogany panelling. Some of the Italians who helped create City Hall's renowned marbled interiors (built with marble from the Greek quarry that supplied classical Greece and Rome) also worked on the great Harland & Wolff liners.

But by far the most poignant connection with the doomed ship is the start of this walk, the Titanic Memorial Garden in the grounds of City Hall. The garden was created in 2012, the centenary of *Titanic*'s sinking, around

LEGEND

1. City Hall, Titanic Memorial Garden – Start
2. Freemasons Hall
3. Morning Star
4. Royal Courts of Justice
5. Belfast Waterfront
6. Belfast Barge
7. Thanksgiving Beacon
8. Footbridge across the Lagan
9. Big Fish
10. Donegall Quay
11. St Joseph's Church
12. Mural, Short Street
13. Clarendon Dock
14. City Quays
15. Clarendon Graving Dock

16. Belfast Harbour Commissioner's Office
17. Sinclair Seamen's Presbyterian Church
18. Custom House Square
19. McHugh's Bar
20. Odyssey Complex
21. SSE Arena

DOCK ST

GARMOYLE ST

SHORT ST

PRINCE'S DOCK ST

PILOT ST

CORPORATION ST

CORPORATION SQUARE

RIVER LAGAN

SYDENHAM RD

QUEEN'S SQUARE

FOOTBRIDGE

QUEEN'S QUAY

WILLIAM ST SOUTH

ANN ST

QUEEN'S BRIDGE

DONEGALL PLACE

ARTHUR ST

VICTORIA ST

WELLINGTON PLACE

CHICHESTER ST

DONEGALL SQ WEST

DONEGALL SQ EAST

MONTGOMERY ST

The *Titanic* Memorial at Belfast City Hall, commemorating all who died in the RMS *Titanic* disaster.

the original Titanic Memorial: a marble figure of Thane, sculpted by Thomas Brock, with two sea nymphs holding an anonymous drowned man. Bronze plaques in the small garden list all 1512 victims of the disaster: the only memorial in the world to do so.

From here we walk over to the other side of Donegall Square, to a building Oscar Wilde once described, unfairly, as Belfast's 'only beautiful building'. Initially an 1860s linen warehouse designed by the great Victorian architect of Belfast, Charles Lanyon, it's now a Marks & Spencer outlet. Turn right and walk down Chichester Street.

Pass by Callender Street and take a left at Arthur Street, once under water and where the Donegall family moored their pleasure barges. You will see a few Arthur, Chichester or Donegall street names throughout the city: all refer to the founding father and original landlords of Belfast. Move on to Arthur Square. Once the old Cornmarket, it was here that United Irishman Henry Joy McCracken was hanged in 1798. His sister, feminist pioneer Mary Ann McCracken, vainly arranged for a surgeon to resuscitate her brother in nearby Pottinger's Entry, where the venerable Morning Star Pub was built a decade later.

At 7 Arthur Square you mustn't miss the historic Freemasons Hall, home to generations of Belfast masons. Veer around William Street to the right, circling the vast new Victoria Square shopping centre, and turn right into Montgomery Street.

At the end of Montgomery Street, turn left into Chichester Street. Cross over at the lights at Victoria Street and walk by the extension of Chichester Street past the white Portland stone neo-classical Royal Courts of Justice on your left, trying not to bump into pinstriped solicitors and bewigged barristers hurrying by.

Cross over Oxford Street and head down to the water. Here is the circular Belfast Waterfront, whose opening in 1997 marked the beginning of the city's post-Troubles regeneration. Overlooking the Lagan River, its great copper dome will eventually turn green to match the dome of City Hall and other historic buildings. All kinds of plays, musicals, operas and dance events are hosted here, as well as concerts by the likes of James Galway, Robbie Williams and Tom Jones.

We pick up our nautical theme again just beyond the Waterfront. Moored on the Lagan is the wonderful Belfast Barge. The city's only floating venue, it's an unusual mix of maritime museum and performance space, as well as a restaurant/café. It's run by the Lagan Legacy, a maritime charity whose exhaustive research has resulted in an exhibition – 'The Greatest Story Never Told' – featuring audio interviews with Harland & Wolff workers, rare photographs of the shipyards and port and more.

We continue on to Queen's Bridge, over which generations of shipyard workers would have travelled on trams, past the striking Thanksgiving

A night-time view of the River Lagan where it is crossed by Queen's Bridge.

Beacon (or Beacon of Hope – it has an abundance of names), a large stainless steel and bronze statue of a girl standing on a globe, sensitively nicknamed the 'Belle on the Ball' and the 'Thing with the Ring' by locals. Cross over Queen's Bridge. On the other side you'll see Tedfords, now a popular restaurant, its exterior little changed since it was a Victorian ships' chandlers.

Carry on down, over the Queen Elizabeth II Bridge, a more modern addition than Queen's Bridge.

When you see the Big Fish, a colourful sculpture of ceramic tiles, each of which tells a story of Belfast, on the pedestrianised Donegall Quay, you're seconds away from the excellent *Titanic* boat tour (try it on the way back!). Run by the Lagan Boat Company, it gives visitors a unique waterside view of the Harland & Wolff shipyards. There's a Belfast Bikes stop here too.

Walk on along the river, passing under the flyover. The view of ferries travelling up the Lagan, now at its widest, into Belfast Lough gives just a small indication of what Belfast was like in its heyday. This stretch of the river would once have been heaving with ships, including some emerging from shipyards here.

Across the river looms first the great Odyssey Centre, then, just beyond Hamilton Dock, the distinctive Titanic Belfast visitor centre. We continue along this walkway for some time, enjoying the views, crossing over a small quay, until we reach a block of modern offices (currently the home of the *Belfast Telegraph*) near the end of the walkway.

Cut through the car park here to a square that was once part of Sailortown, the heart of Belfast's sailing fraternity. Unforgivably, this once so important and atmospheric area has received little protection from the planners. Here dockers, sailors and shipbuilders mingled with seafaring folk working on the incoming ships.

We continue down Prince's Dock Street with the remnants of the old tram lines, past the once thriving and now derelict Pat's Bar and the old church that was the spiritual centre of the area, St Joseph's. 'The Church on the Quays' was closed in 2001, despite a long campaign to save it as a community centre.

At the corner of Dock Street, a mural commemorates the dockers who lived and worked here until as late as the 1970s. A newly restored old pub, The American Bar, at 65 Dock Street is worth a detour.

But we turn left at Short Street. At the end of this aptly named street is Belfast's finest mural. Everything you need to know about Sailortown, St Joseph's and the closely knit community that once thronged this area can be found here.

We turn left into Garmoyle Street, which soon becomes Corporation Street. Then we turn left into Clarendon Dock, an upmarket office development. Here, straight ahead, you will find the Clarendon Graving Dock, built by the founder of Belfast's shipbuilding heritage, Scot William Ritchie, in 1800. This is where it all began. Ahead are the docks that were once part of Ritchie McLaine shipbuilders.

You can walk through the car park, following the signs to the Victorian Belfast Harbour Commissioners' Office, where the city's status as a port and world-leading shipbuilding centre was planned. Walk around to the front of the building in Corporation Square.

Belfast originally developed around its port, with its merchants importing goods such as wine and tobacco and exporting butter, beef, grain and timber. But its late Victorian stature as a world-leading port was achieved only after extensive works to deepen what became Victoria Channel, essential for the new generations of ever-larger ships. The reclaimed earth from digging the new channel was the foundation of Queen's Island, where Harland and Wolff later developed their famous shipbuilding business. Those developments were plotted in the Harbour Commissioners' Office. Pre-arranged visits are recommended, not least to view the captain's table in the boardroom that arrived just too late to be installed in *Titanic*.

Just along from here is one of Ireland's most idiosyncratic churches, Sinclair Seamen's Presbyterian Church, open to visitors on Wednesday afternoons. Designed, inevitably, by Charles Lanyon, in the 1850s, its pitch pine pulpit is in the shape of a ship's prow with navigation lights on each side, while service is called by a bell from HMS *Hood*. Several other nautical touches reveal that its congregation once included many visiting sailors.

From the Belfast Harbour Commissioners Office, we circle left around Donegall Quay, walking under the flyover on our way back. Soon we pass the Obel Tower, within which is the office of the Lagan Boat Company, which also has some unique nautical items for sale. Why not buy a ticket for its *Titanic* tour here if you have time?

Across the road from here is the impressive Palladian Customs House, where novelist Anthony Trollope worked in the 1850s (need one point out at this stage that it was designed by Charles Lanyon?). It was Trollope who introduced letterboxes to Britain. Behind it is Custom House Square, Belfast's answer to London's Speakers' Corner, as signified by the life-size bronze statue, *The Speaker*. Here the famous trade unionist Jim Larkin addressed 20,000 workers during the Belfast dockers' strike of 1907. It's now a regular performance place and venue for various festivals.

Fountains here mark the line of the Farset river, now underground, which once flowed down High Street. This is more or less where Belfast started. Béal Feirste, the Irish for Belfast, means 'the mouth of the sand bank ford'. That was roughly here, where the river Lagan meets the river Farset.

Here too, in what was once the city's red-light district, is the site of Belfast's oldest building, now McHugh's Bar. This one-time bordello has been beautifully restored and is worth a visit in itself for its many historical features and mementos and some good pub grub.

Along Donegall Quay is the footbridge across the Lagan that leads into Titanic Quarter. Walk along, past the Odyssey Complex, a multi-attraction pavilion adjacent to the SSE Arena, home to the Belfast Giants ice-hockey team and large-scale concerts. We follow Sydenham Road around to the Hamilton Dock. This is the beginning of Titanic Quarter, a huge development based around the former Harland & Wolff docks with many *Titanic* connections.

We continue our exploration of Titanic Quarter on another walk.

Distance: 4 km (2.5 miles)
Average time: 90 minutes
Starts at: City Hall

18.

City Hall to Queen's Quarter

T his walk takes us through the city centre, past the venerable Ulster Hall, along bohemian Botanic Avenue to Queen's University, the lovely Botanic Gardens and its spectacular Palm House, the Ulster Museum, Belfast's most ancient graveyard and back.

We start outside Visit Belfast (Belfast's main tourist information centre), opposite City Hall on Donegall Square North. Turn to your right and walk down about fifty yards until you reach the elegant columned entrance to the Linen Hall Library. It's a wonderful place to while away a few hours, so be careful if you detour here! The last public subscription library left in Ireland, it has played a major part in Belfast's cultural life for over two centuries. It's been housed in this former linen warehouse only since the late 1890s, but there's an air of timelessness from the moment you ascend its brass-railed staircase to enjoy its three floors of wooden

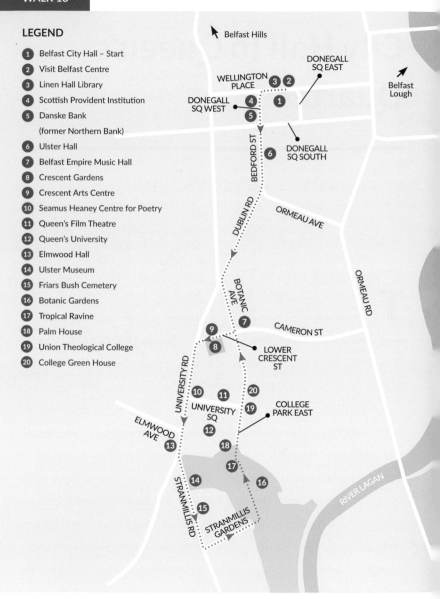

LEGEND

1. Belfast City Hall – Start
2. Visit Belfast Centre
3. Linen Hall Library
4. Scottish Provident Institution
5. Danske Bank
   (former Northern Bank)
6. Ulster Hall
7. Belfast Empire Music Hall
8. Crescent Gardens
9. Crescent Arts Centre
10. Seamus Heaney Centre for Poetry
11. Queen's Film Theatre
12. Queen's University
13. Elmwood Hall
14. Ulster Museum
15. Friars Bush Cemetery
16. Botanic Gardens
17. Tropical Ravine
18. Palm House
19. Union Theological College
20. College Green House

bookcases stacked with, among others, the finest Irish studies collection in Northern Ireland. Beloved of Seamus Heaney and many other literary figures, it is also famous for an unrivalled Troubles collection.

Cross over Wellington Place at the lights and walk down Donegall Square West. The dominant building on this side is the vast sandstone Scottish Provident Institution, which is nearly as grand as City Hall opposite. This venerable building once housed Belfast's main contribution to the detective genre, the company that made the distinctive Ulster coat, as worn by Sherlock Holmes. Have a good look at the building as you pass: high up are examples of a popular local art form, stone carvings. They adorn several of Belfast's finest buildings and here show cherubs working on a printing press, as well as an anchor and hammer representing shipbuilding and yarn and a spinning wheel for the linen and ropemaking industries.

A little further down the street, now the Danske Bank, at the corner of Donegall Square West and Wellington Street, is the former Northern Bank which achieved great fame in 2004 following a £26 million cash robbery, the biggest in UK history. It nearly destabilised the then still fragile peace process, as there were (unsubstantiated) rumours of republican involvement.

Cross over Wellington Street to Bedford Street and cross over at the lights to the left-hand side of the street. It's an interesting street with one of Belfast's most historic buildings – the Ulster Hall – a little further down. Take a tour inside if you have time. Restored a few years ago, the two-storey Italianate building began life as a grand ballroom in 1862, becoming at one point the largest music hall in the British Isles. Stand in the main hall, admiring the vast Mulholland organ, and imagine witnessing such disparate talents as Charles Dickens, Paul Robeson, Caruso, Sir Edward Elgar, the Rolling Stones and Led Zeppelin, who debuted 'Stairway to Heaven' here. Charles Stewart Parnell, Patrick Pearse and David Lloyd George held rallies here.

At the corner of Bedford Street and Ormeau Avenue, a red granite drinking fountain commemorates Thomas Thompson, a local pioneer against diseases such as cholera. This area, outside the BBC offices, might be familiar to regular viewers of Northern Irish news due to the many interviews conducted here.

Cross over Ormeau Avenue and head down the Dublin Road, once fancifully named the 'Golden Mile'. Ethnic eateries and cheery bars can't disguise a rather down-at-heel look. But keep walking, crossing Donegall Avenue (a loyalist enclave with several murals where two or three shops survive of what was Belfast's antique heartland) and you will find that cosmopolitan Botanic Avenue is of more interest.

With the large student population on its doorstep, it's little wonder that Botanic Avenue is one of the city's liveliest streets. The tree-lined avenue is packed with interesting cafés and delis and even boasts a famed crime bookshop. Its great attraction is the Belfast Empire Music Hall. Having begun life as a Presbyterian church in 1870s, it was over a century later that it took on its current role as a bar with live entertainment. Ghostbusters were called in when the upstairs was converted into a music-hall-style theatre and staff believed the ghosts of the original elders were wreaking revenge for the alcohol now sold on church premises. Renowned for its comedy, the Empire has also featured leading Irish music acts such as Snow Patrol.

Now cross Botanic Avenue and take a right down Lower Crescent Street, past the Georgian Crescent Townhouse to the Crescent Arts Centre at the junction with University Road. Once a pioneer of women's education, this beautifully restored Scrabo stone 1870s building now houses one of the city's most comprehensive arts centres.

Continue up University Road past the lovely Crescent Church until you reach University Square. At the corner here is the Seamus Heaney Centre

Queen's University, designed by the Belfast's most famous architect, Charles Lanyon.

for Poetry, a regular venue for literary readings and talks. At the other end of University Square, facing Queen's University, is the Queen's Film Theatre (No. 20), the city's best showcase for world cinema.

Cross University Street and on your left is the main entrance to red-brick Queen's University, designed in the Tudor style by Charles Lanyon, whose name this main building bears. Enquire at the visitor centre here for a guided tour, which includes the Oxbridge-modelled Great Hall. Also here is the Naughton Gallery, which showcases the university's impressive art collection. On leafy Elmwood Avenue opposite is the impressive Scrabo sandstone Elmwood Hall, once a Presbyterian church and now a concert venue. The excellent University Bookshop is next door. Further down Elmwood Avenue is the Catholic Chaplaincy, where poet Philip Larkin, once a lecturer here, wrote some of his most famous poetry.

Continue until you reach the entrance to the Botanic Gardens and veer right to the Ulster Museum if you have time for a quick (free) visit. Reopened in 2009 after a very expensive renovation, this has long been one of the city's most popular destinations. Edmontosaurus, the most complete dinosaur fossil on display on the island of Ireland, stands at the foot of the display tower in the atrium, vying with Eygptian princess Takabuti, the first mummy to be displayed outside Egypt, as the museum's main attraction for kids. She's known as 'Belfast's oldest bleached blonde' due to her chemically discoloured hair. It's the best place to get an understanding of the city's industrial heritage, part of many of our walks, as well as Irish history, and you can also explore its excellent art gallery.

Turn left outside the museum and take the exit into Stranmillis Road, walking uphill until you reach the entrance to Friar's Bush Cemetery, which dates from a sixteenth-century friary (not the tombstone mischievously marked 483AD). The cemetery takes its evocative name from the Penal Era of persecution in the eighteenth century, when the city's then tiny Catholic community worshipped furtively here beneath an old thorn bush in the centre of the graveyard. The central mound here marks the site of a medieval church of St Patrick, while just inside the walls a plaque records the site of a mass grave where 800 fever victims died during the Great Famine.

Return to the entrance to the cemetery and continue until you reach Stranmillis Gardens, which leads back into the Botanic Gardens. Head towards the signposted Tropical Ravine. Built in 1889, it's like a mini-rainforest with all kinds of exotic plants, and well worth a diversion. The sunken ravine can be viewed from balconies at each end. The park's other attraction is the delightful Palm House, one of the earliest examples of a curvilinear cast-iron glasshouse in the world. It was built

The Palm House in the Botanic Gardens, one of the earliest examples of a curvilinear cast-iron glasshouse in the world.

by Richard Turner four years before he turned his attention to a larger version at Kew Gardens in London. The Palm House has a cool wing and a tropical wing, which features the impressive dome. Beyond the Palm House the north gate leads on to College Park East.

Head down this road on the right-hand side, passing the imposing classical Union Theological College, just after University Avenue. Designed, inevitably, by Charles Lanyon, it was once home to the Northern Ireland Parliament. Just further on is Molly's Yard, a restaurant serving local craft ales. It is housed in a coach house of the 1870 College Green House, which boasts several illustrious former inhabitants, including the late playwright Stewart Parker. It featured in the film of local writer Colin Bateman's novel *Divorcing Jack*. Bateman is one of the authors featured in No Alibis, a specialist crime bookshop situated on the left-hand side of Botanic Avenue.

From here, you can either retrace your steps to the city centre or get a Metro bus.

Distance: 2.4 km (1.5 miles)
Average time: 90 minutes (ending at Botanic Avenue)
Start at: City Hall

19.

City Hall to Cathedral Quarter

T his walk takes us through the history of Belfast, encountering revolutionaries, ancient pubs, blind harpists, famous delis and the earliest days of the city.

We start at City Hall. It was built to impress, and it still does. The building was conceived after Queen Victoria afforded city status in 1888 to Belfast, then a leader in myriad industries from linen and ropemaking to shipbuilding and tobacco. The unionist elite who ran the city set their sights on a suitably imposing headquarters to reflect their importance. In the event, architect Alfred Brunwell Thomas's masterpiece went massively over budget, but it was worth it. Check out the spectacular reception halls, overlaid with marble from the quarry that supplied classical Greece and Rome.

We start at the main entrance to City Hall, facing Donegall Place. Cross over Donegall Square, turn left past the Visit Belfast centre and

LEGEND

1. City Hall
2. Linen Hall Library
3. Sawers Deli
4. St Mary's Chapel
5. Kelly's Cellars
6. Bank Square
7. Rosemary Street First Presbyterian Church
8. White's Tavern, Winecellar Entry
9. Royal Exchange Building
10. John Hewitt bar
11. St Anne's Cathedral
12. Merchant Hotel
13. St George's Church
14. Albert Memorial Clock
15. Malmaison Hotel
16. Bittles Bar
17. Jaffe Memorial fountain
18. St George's Market

East Belfast

VICTORIA ST

MAY ST

SKIPPER ST

HILL ST

WARING ST

TALBOT ST

ROSEMARY ST

DONEGALL ST

CASTLE PLACE

DONEGALL SQUARE

ROYAL AVENUE

CASTLE ST

FOUNTAIN ST

COLLEGE ST

NORTH ST

QUEEN ST

CHAPEL LANE

Belfast Hills

The atmospheric Linen Hall Library, loved by Seamus Heaney, has barely changed in over a century.

walk on until you come to the main entrance to the Linen Hall Library This wonderfully atmospheric building, with its winding stairs, wooden bookcases and stained-glass windows, houses Ireland's only public subscription library. Its Irish studies collection and exhibition dedicated to the Troubles alone make a visit worthwhile. It was designed by the architect of much of Victorian Belfast, Charles Lanyon. A founder member of the original library (then situated in Ann Street) was Thomas Russell of the revolutionary Society of United Irishmen. Another member was his friend Henry Joy McCracken, leader of the northern rebels, executed in the 1798 Rising. Henry Joy's unpaid library fine was paid by a relative only a few years ago! The library remains a venue for all kinds of cultural activities today.

Turn right just beyond the library into Fountain Street and first left into College Street. Here you'll pass Belfast's oldest and most famous deli, Sawers. Once it provided the Harland & Wolff offices where *Titanic* was designed with game, poultry and cheeses. Established back in 1897, it moved here in the 1980s and has become renowned for not just all kinds of local delicacies but exotic meats like zebra, kangaroo, camel and rattlesnake too.

At the end of College Street turn right into Queen Street and cross over Castle Street into Chapel Lane. Walk along to the delightful St Mary's Chapel, the first Catholic church to be built in Belfast (in 1784). In those surprisingly enlightened times, when Belfast was known as the 'Athens of the North', it was partly paid for by Presbyterians. Given Belfast's subsequent history, it remains a tangible sign of what might have been, and what could still be.

With your back to St Mary's, you're facing Bank Square and in sight of one of Belfast's oldest pubs, Kelly's Cellars. Here, Henry Joy McCracken hid under the counter as English soldiers pursued him in 1798. This area was once populated by a group called the fadgies (from the Irish *A Pháidí* – vocative case of 'Paddy' – the term they called each other). Irish speakers from Omeath, by Carlingford Lough, they sold oysters from the lough, fish, seafood and fruit and vegetables around Belfast from the 1840s.

Head past Kelly's around Bank Street to Royal Avenue. Renamed for Queen Victoria, this was once the 'street of the butchers', when it was known as Hercules Street and over fifty butchers had their premises here. Look to your right to the adjacent Tesco supermarket in what was the nineteenth-century Provincial Bank and the impressive five-storey red sandstone building next to it now inhabited by Primark. The two buildings give you an idea of what this central part of Belfast looked like in its Victorian pomp.

Castle Street, in which Primark stands, and nearby Castle Place, neither prepossessing, are, however, of significance. It was here that the first Belfast Castle stood. Sir Arthur Chichester, founder of the Donegall dynasty and kindly termed an adventurer (actually a ruthless murderer), built up the city from this castle in the early 1600s.

Cross over the road to Rosemary Street with its charming reminder of Belfast's golden age, the First Presbyterian Church. Dating from 1781 and the city's oldest surviving place of worship, its boat-like interior must have pleased regular attender Thomas Andrews, the designer of *Titanic*. Henry Joy McCracken and his family also worshipped here in earlier times. The famous actress Sarah Siddons played at the eighteenth-century Playhouse across the road (the building sadly no longer exists). This was once the sweetest smelling street in Belfast – not a great boast then, admittedly – as it was packed with herb gardens.

As we walk along, take a look into Winecellar Entry (entry is Belfast-speak for lane) on the right, where Belfast's oldest continuously licensed premises, White's, can be found. It has been rebuilt several times since 1630.

Cross over North Street to its junction with Waring Street. You are standing outside one of Belfast's most historic buildings, the Royal Exchange. Built by Lord Donegall in 1769 as the Market House, a second floor was added later as the Assembly Rooms. The most fashionable venue for dances and entertainment, it was here that Edward Bunting, adopted brother to Henry Joy McCracken, held a festival of blind harpists in 1792 that is credited with saving Irish music. All mileage from Belfast was calculated from here, highlighting the importance of this area to early Belfast.

Walk around the building and turn left into Donegall Street. Cross over and head up Donegall Road towards St Anne's Cathedral. You're now in the heart of the Cathedral Quarter. Named for St Anne's, its cobbled streets, old warehouses and red-brick buildings have been developed as Belfast's answer to Dublin's Temple Bar, a mix of cultural attractions, traditional pubs, restaurants and clubs. This was once Belfast's version of Fleet Street, and the *Belfast Telegraph* and *Irish News* are just up past St Anne's. Look right as you pass Commercial Court, a pleasant alleyway in which the Duke of York, long a journalists' favourite, remains popular. It was here that a young Gerry Adams pulled pints in the 1960s.

Still walking down Donegall Street, you come to the John Hewitt bar, a focus of cultural events also renowned for good gastro fare and local brews. It is named after the Belfast poet and socialist and owned by the Belfast Unemployed Resource Centre, so the profits from your pint go to a good cause.

Cross Talbot Street to the Church of Ireland St Anne's Cathedral or Belfast Cathedral. Although opened in 1904, it wasn't officially completed until its spectacular forty-metre steel spire was added in 2007. It's worth a detour inside if you have time, especially the roof of the baptistery, which has over 150,000 pieces of glass that took two English sisters, Gertrude and Madge Martin, five years to complete.

Walk back around Talbot Street, passing the Northern Ireland War Memorial Exhibition and turning right into the cobblestoned Hill Street, perhaps the heart of the Cathedral Quarter. Known for its listed brick and stucco warehouses, it's full of interesting pubs, restaurants and even a tea room decorated with antiques from the *Titanic* era.

From Hill Street we emerge back into Waring Street. Named after a successful tanner, William Waring, this is one of Belfast's oldest streets and was long a street of commerce. Its finest building can be seen across the road from here. Housed in the 1860s former Ulster Bank, with its elaborate cast-iron balustrade, is the five-star Merchant Hotel, renowned for the theatrical splendour of its dining room in the old banking hall where Ireland's largest chandelier hangs from a glass dome.

The Merchant Hotel in Waring Street, converted from the magnificent 1860s Ulster Bank building.

It is said that the street before us used to be cobbled with wood so the passing horses and carts wouldn't be too noisy and annoy the bank staff trying to count money. William Waring has another claim to fame, by the way. His daughter, Jane, rejected Jonathan Swift's proposal of marriage when he was living in nearby Carrickfergus. He later immortalised her in literature as Varina.

Continue across to Skipper Street, named for the sea captains who took lodgings here while their boats were moored in what is now High Street. Now culverted beneath, the Farset river once flowed along High Street.

Across the road is St George's Church, which roughly marks the birth-place of Belfast. The church dates from the early 1800s but a chapel stood here many centuries before. Its classical portico was brought from the eccentric Earl Bishop of Derry's unfinished house. From here you can see another famous Belfast landmark, the Albert Memorial, once known as the 'leaning tower of Belfast'. Built on reclaimed land on the spot where Queen Victoria and Prince Albert landed when they visited the city, its famous list was corrected in recent times.

Turn right into Victoria Street. Across the road you will see the Malmaison Hotel. There were once two seed warehouses here, Lyttle's on the left and McCausland's. Like many Belfast buildings, it is covered in carvings. A native American, English gent, turbaned Indian and others highlight the company's trade with the five continents.

Further on, past the city's famous triangular pub, Bittles, is the entrance to the new Victoria Square shopping centre and the Jaffe Memorial fountain. Venture into the former if you want spectacular views of Belfast from its glass dome. The fountain is dedicated to German Daniel Jaffe, who was a kind of unofficial head of Belfast's once thriving Jewish community. His son Otto, who inherited the family's linen business, became Lord Mayor of Belfast twice.

One of the lesser-known industries in which Belfast was a world leader was soft drinks. One of the reasons lies under this shopping centre – Cromac Springs. Companies like Grattan's, Cantrell & Cochrane's and Ross's used Belfast's supply of spring water to produce tonic water and ginger ale for the world. Thomas Cantrell introduced Club Soda, while Canada Dry Ginger Ale began life as Belfast-style ginger ale.

Keep on going down Victoria Street. Across the road from here is a red-brick building which was once Belfast Town Hall (itself built over the old pork market). Even as it opened, Belfast Corporation (Belfast City Council) realised it was too small, and within a few years was building City Hall around the corner.

When Belfast began to develop in the early 1600s, it was the food merchants who contributed most to the city's growth, exporting local produce like beef, corn and butter, and importing foreign goods like sugarcane, wine and brandy. From its first Market House in 1664, Belfast has been famous for its wonderful food markets.

At the junction with May Street, cross over Victoria Street and continue up May Street until you come to the entrance to the longest surviving covered food market in Ireland. The beautifully restored St George's Market is renowned for its variety of wonderful local produce, including fish and seafood, gourmet homemade sausages, organic meats and vegetables, Irish cheeses and even highly prized local seaweed. It hosts the Friday Variety Market, the multi-award winning Saturday Food and Garden Market and the most recent addition, the Sunday Market.

Now it's time to return to City Hall. Turn left into May Street and walk down all the way. En route you will pass Nos 38 to 42, where veterinary surgeon John Boyd Dunlop invented the first successful pneumatic tyre, and the attractive Victorian home of auctioneers Ross & Co. at Nos 22–26.

Distance: 1.9 km (1.2 miles)
Average time: 1 hour
Starts at: City Hall

20.

Stormont Estate

You'll recognise that distinctive mile-long, tree-lined avenue leading up to the Parliament Buildings at Stormont from a thousand news reports of the Troubles. It's been the home of the Northern Irish government since 1932 and of the Assembly since 2007. What you might not realise is that the estate here offers one of Belfast's most beautiful walks, so why leave it to the politicians?

The original estate, known as Storm Mount because of its windy, exposed location, was established by a local rector in 1830. His modest family home was redesigned as a baronial castle in the 1850s and the grounds enhanced. It was bought by the Northern Ireland government in 1921, after the partition of Ireland, when the Parliament Buildings were commissioned by George V. Tours of the building have to be arranged through the MLAs (elected representatives) themselves, but you will be allowed into the magnificent marbled Great Hall, where most of Northern Ireland's political press conferences are held. At the top of the stairs is a statue of Sir James Craig, Northern Ireland's first Prime Minister. The building also contains his tomb.

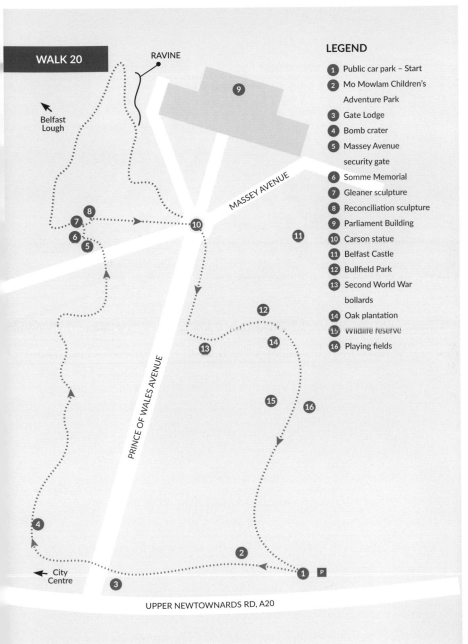

WALK 20

RAVINE

Belfast
Lough

MASSEY AVENUE

PRINCE OF WALES AVENUE

City
Centre

UPPER NEWTOWNARDS RD, A20

LEGEND

1. Public car park – Start
2. Mo Mowlam Children's Adventure Park
3. Gate Lodge
4. Bomb crater
5. Massey Avenue security gate
6. Somme Memorial
7. Gleaner sculpture
8. Reconciliation sculpture
9. Parliament Building
10. Carson statue
11. Belfast Castle
12. Bullfield Park
13. Second World War bollards
14. Oak plantation
15. Wildlife reserve
16. Playing fields

Stormont Parliament Buildings.

The castle isn't open to the public at all, but its turrets and buildings can be glimpsed through the trees at various points. There are some interesting historic sites along the way, as well as picnic and barbeque facilities, so this is not a walk to hurry.

We start at the public car park. We are taking the 'Long Woodland Walk', the longest of the three allegedly waymarked walks. In truth, the signposting is sparse, to put it kindly. Most of the first half of the walk, however, is made easy by the fact that we follow the nearest path to the edge of the estate, always on our left.

From the car park, you can see the Parliament Building high up ahead in the distance and, to its left, the turrets of Stormont Castle. Now, follow the path past the Mo Mowlam Children's Park, named after the former

Secretary of State for Northern Ireland, who suggested it. Staying on the left, we cross over the great central thoroughfare, Prince of Wales Avenue, from near the Gate Lodge. Over the avenue, we take the left-hand path now at all times, skirting first the road and then a series of private buildings on the other side of the fence as we circle right and start the uphill trek through the trees.

We soon pass a large crater, left by a German bomb during the Second World War. In 1941, Belfast suffered horrifically from Luftwaffe bombing, not least because increased wartime production at the Harland & Wolff shipyard, which was nearly destroyed, made it an important target. War will be a continuing theme of the monuments we encounter.

Keeping to the left at all times, you will come to a plantation of giant Scots pine. Soon our path winds around to the left even more as a wooden fenced path zigzags over some marshy ground through the pines. We are fairly close now to the very edge of the estate. Cross a wooden bridge and keep straight on. Resist the temptation to join the open land you glimpse to your right, and keep on the path nearest the exterior of the estate.

Not too far away you come to a fork in the path and, for once, you take a right, walking around the white building you will have glimpsed through the trees. To your right you will notice the central avenue heading uphill on an ever-rising bank. Circle around, enjoying your first relatively close views of the vast Parliament Buildings. Head towards the Massey Avenue security gate (near the entrance here), past a toilet block. Over the road, near the security entrance, a path leads upwards through the grass.

On your left, a short path takes you to the Somme Memorial (a large piece of granite) and its surrounding cedar trees. The Battle of the Somme, in which the 36th Ulster Division suffered particularly badly in the first two days alone, has an iconic status among unionists, though it should be remembered that many nationalists died in the long battle too.

Return the short distance to the path you were on. At its end is the Gleaner sculpture. This was sculpted by John Knox for the Festival of Britain in 1951 and shows a woman on bended knee with the inscription, 'Thrift is the gleaner behind all human effort.'

If you want to walk further upwards to view the ravine, turn right at the Gleaner statue and then left. This will give you great views of the side of the Parliament Building from across the ever-deepening ravine too. If not, instead of turning left, continue on the pathway which takes you around to the Reconciliation sculpture. Set amid two little ponds, this depicts a man and woman embracing each other across barbed wire. It was inspired by a woman's quest to find her husband after the Second World War. Identical statues were presented to other cities that suffered wartime bombing: Coventry, Hiroshima and Berlin.

Walk diagonally across the grass to Massey Avenue, the Parliament Building now looming large to your left. At the roundabout is the famous twelve-foot statue of Edward Carson. Carson, who is buried in the grounds, was the leader of unionism in the years before partition, though a divided Ireland was never his intention and he consequently turned down the chance to be first Prime Minister of Northern Ireland. He is also known as the prosecution barrister who destroyed Oscar Wilde.

Now walk down the Prince of Wales Avenue before turning left about halfway down (the first left-hand turn). Before the path circles around to the left, past a toilet block, are some Second World War bollards. These were used to hold barrage balloons which defended the Parliament Buildings, then covered in camouflage paint.

The path turns right soon, passing the Bullfield park before turning right again by an oak plantation. From here you largely keep the playing fields and artificial pitches to your left as you continue past the wildlife reserve on your right. You will pass some woodland on your right and eventually a picnic area behind fencing before arriving back at the car park.

Distance: 4 km (2.5 miles)

Average time: 80 minutes

Public transport: Metro 20A or 23 from city centre (Donegall Square West).

By car: From the Upper Newtownards Road (coming from the city centre) pass the main entrance and turn left at the traffic lights into the car park, about 250 metres further on.

21.

Minnowburn and the Giant's Ring

One of several excellent walks that lead off from the Lagan Towpath, this National Trust trail takes us back to the Neolithic age and Belfast of the 1930s. But the overarching sense is actually one of timelessness as you traipse through countryside of such tranquillity that it's impossible to believe you're within a few miles of a busy city centre.

The circular walk starts in Minnowburn Car Park, just a short stroll across Shaw's Bridge from Barnett Demesne and our main Lagan Towpath walk. You could just as easily park at Shaw's Bridge, cross the old stone bridge and walk along the towpath from there to the starting point.

At the small Minnowburn Car Park you will see a large noticeboard. Alongside is a series of steps leading down to the towpath. Turn left here and walk by the river as it meanders around. Approximately 250 metres on you will come to some finger-posts. Take the direction towards Giant's Ring, turning left and upwards along the path.

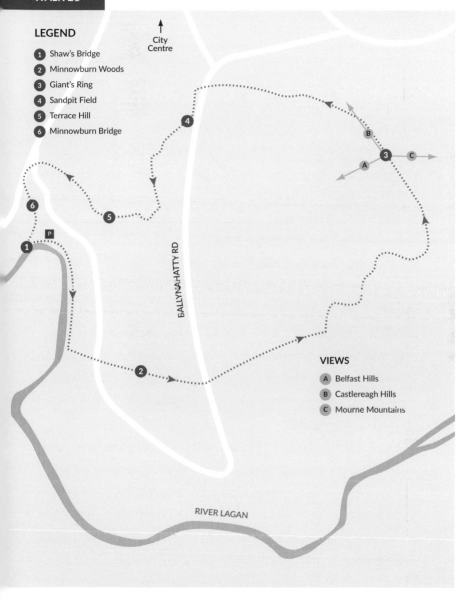

LEGEND

1. Shaw's Bridge
2. Minnowburn Woods
3. Giant's Ring
4. Sandpit Field
5. Terrace Hill
6. Minnowburn Bridge

City Centre

BALLYNAHATTY RD

VIEWS

A. Belfast Hills
B. Castlereagh Hills
C. Mourne Mountains

RIVER LAGAN

Fairly soon you will come to Edenderry Road. Cross over, enter the gate, which is nearly opposite, and walk up the narrow path with woodland on either side. These are Minnowburn Woods, which include the towering Minnowburn Beeches. Most of the older trees here, generally beech, date just from the 1960s and the newer ones are very recent. These include oak, ash and hazel. The oak trees were grown from acorns taken from the ancient trees in Belvoir Forest Park (another dedicated walk in this book) and therefore descended from the ancient forests of Ireland.

Keep following the finger-post signs for Giant's Ring (ignore signs for Terrace Hill Garden at this stage). When you reach the top of the next stile in this part, look back to enjoy glorious views of Malone House and the Belfast Hills framed behind (however, save time for the views from the Giant's Ring, which are truly spectacular).

Cross over Ballynahatty Road and enter the gate over the road (you'll recognise the National Trust logo) by a cottage. A narrow path leads uphill through rolling green fields by hedgerows emblazoned with yellow gorse. We continue on this path for some time. The paths on this walk do become quite muddy after rain, so boots are highly recommended. Occasional glimpses of buildings aside, this remains a quite idyllic rural experience.

Eventually, following the signs, you will come to a green gate. You've reached the famous Giant's Ring, not unlike a prehistoric golfing green, if you can imagine such a thing. Were it, say, three miles outside London, this magnificent site – one of the finest Neolithic henge monuments in the UK or Ireland – would be regularly thronged, but there are times outside summer when you might be alone with your thoughts here.

Inside the huge green ring (approximately 180 metres across) is a passage tomb which consists of five stones and a capstone. Built around 2700 BC,

The Giant's Ring.

thus predating the Pyramids, it may have had several functions, though most likely it was a memorial to the dead. Circle the earthen bank for spectacular views around the Lagan Valley and imagine the kind of activity you might have seen here 4000 years ago.

Walk down the road from the car park on the other side of the Giant's Ring. A gate here is locked (ring for opening times) from different hours in summer and winter. Turn left, watching for traffic, and then take a right over the road, where you will see a finger-post directing you towards Terrace Hill Garden. This takes you into a field.

Turn left and walk around the exterior of the field (if weather conditions don't permit, the adjoining road will do as well, as long as you keep to the exterior on the other side). This is the Sandpit Field, where the views are particularly stunning. In 1969 this natural amphitheatre was the venue for a pop concert convened to unite young Catholics and Protestants.

The 18th-century Minnowburn Bridge, at the end of this walk.

Unfortunately it coincided with violence that spread throughout the city, ushering in the Troubles.

Stay close to the left-hand side of the field, and when you are near the bottom you will see a stile with a wooden finger-post for Terrace Hill Garden. Climb over the stile, cross the road and take the path on the other side, leading upwards to Terrace Hill Garden. As you circle around at the top you will see a Native American totem pole. You will want to continue on the path to the right of this, where a finger-post directs you back to the Minnowburn Car Park.

But first, take a little time to explore the Art Deco Rose Garden to your left here and its beautiful view of Malone House. The garden was created by the wealthy Edward 'Ned' Robinson, who built the nearby house (still privately owned) in 1936 and used the garden for musical parties which attracted the elite of Belfast society of the day. Now managed by the National Trust, it still stages occasional live music events.

Head on around the totem, turning left at the sign for the car park. Enjoy an unusual view of the twin icons of the Belfast skyline, the Harland & Wolff cranes Samson and Goliath, as you wander around to the car park, crossing over the eighteenth-century Minnowburn Bridge.

Distance: 3.4 km (2.1 miles)

Average time: 70 minutes

Public transport: Ulsterbus 13 from Europa Bus Station to Ramada Hotel. Ulsterbus 13A/B also from Europa Bus Station to Belvoir Park View or Metro 77/78 from Wellington Place to Belvoir Park View – approx. 5 mins walk from this stop.

By car: Minnowburn is just off the A55 Ring Road, next to Shaw's bridge. Follow the signs to Minnowburn Car Park.

22.

Belvoir Forest Park

Back in 1722, Sir Arthur Hill-Trevor, later Viscount Dungannon, bought some 475 acres of Lagan Valley and created a beautiful demesne in the grounds, which already contained oak trees several decades old. As a result, this glorious forest park, managed by the Forest Service since 1961, is home to some of the oldest oak trees in Ireland. Sir Arthur, who became Chancellor of the Irish Exchequer, had an even more distinguished grandson, the Duke of Wellington. The 'Iron Duke' is said to have played in the now destroyed family pile, Belvoir (pronounced Beaver) House, as a child.

The park is the only one in Northern Ireland that is also a commercial forestry, and has a fabulous variety of trees. Thanks to its plentiful birdlife – some thirty-five species of birds have been recorded here, including song thrush, jays and long-eared owls – the RSPB has established its HQ in the park. This is a very scenic walk, with several interesting historical features along the way.

The first of these features is soon encountered. At the top end of the car park, where the views of the Belfast Hills are particularly striking, is a

WALK 22

LEGEND

1. Car park – Start and finish
2. RSPB HQ
3. Norman motte
4. Ice House
5. Scots pines
6. Ancient graveyard
7. Arboretum
8. Wooden bridge
9. Belvoir Park Golf Club
10. Moreland's Meadow
11. Lagan Meadows

noticeboard and a path heading downwards. Take this, and before you on the right as you circle to the left is a series of steep steps leading to a high mount with commanding views of the landscape. This earth mound was a motte. Atop it once was a bailey, a timber fort. It dates from soon after Anglo-Norman John de Courcy's 1177 invasion of Ulster. Be careful not to lose your footing if you decide to ascend, but if you do brave the climb, imagine the Norman soldiers scanning the Lagan below and the surrounding countryside for signs of local Gaelic resistance.

Return carefully down the steps and turn right, following the Lagan river. The old Ice House, situated on a slope of the motte (and possibly to blame for the displacement of the bailey), adjoining the river, was like a large pre-electric version of a fridge. Most is below ground to ensure more consistent temperatures when the interior was packed with ice from the frozen river to keep food fresh.

Cross over a stream here and turn left under a large pipe. The wooded glades throughout this walk, like those you see here, are lovely. Signposting in this park can be a little sparse, but follow the red arrows marked on wooden poles where you see them and you will be all right.

You will soon find yourself walking alongside the Lagan, perhaps at its most idyllic spot. Across the water is Moreland's Meadow, an island formed by the divergence of the Lagan river and canal, where oak and cedar trees abound.

There are quite a few steep inclines on this walk, by the way, so be prepared. The path continues until beyond the end of Moreland's Meadow to the left. Ignore any un-arrowed paths to the right. Eventually the path leaves the river and circles around to a plantation of Scots pine. It gets hilly here as you pass the maze of trees to your right.

After a fairly steep incline, the sight of metal railings announces the beginning of the prestigious Belvoir Park Golf Club. Soon enough you will

Bridge to Belvoir Forest Park.

encounter a small wall probably dating from the fifteenth century. Here is the now empty Dungannon family vault where Sir Arthur was buried. Turn right at the red arrow and wander down. After a while you will encounter a wide variety of trees, including redwood and cedar, in the arboretum first created by Sir Arthur Hill-Trevor.

Cross the wooden bridge and take a path to your left to return to the car park.

Distance: 2.3 km (1.4 miles)
Average time: 45–55 minutes
Public transport: Metro 77 and 78 from city centre (Wellington Place) stop on Belvoir Drive, just opposite the main entrance. Ulsterbus service 13 calls less often at the same stopping point.
By car: From Belvoir Drive, off the A55 outer ring road, a tarmac entrance road leads to the main car park. It is never shut.

23.

Barnett Demesne

Set in acres of beautiful meadows and trees at the heart of the Lagan Valley Regional Park, this is one of Belfast's loveliest spots and offers a tranquil if rather hilly walk. It begins at the elegant Georgian Malone House.

The park gets its name from the last owner of what was an extensive estate, William Barnett, who donated the land and Malone House to the people of Belfast in 1946. He is equally famous locally as the owner of the first Irish horse to win the English Derby (in 1929), Trigo.

Malone House was built in the 1820s by a successful Belfast merchant called William Legge. It was later owned by the Harberton family, after whom the main room (used for all kinds of events) is named. There's always an art exhibition at the Higgin Gallery on the first floor, and the Malone Room is a popular place for coffee, snacks and meals.

We start outside Malone House. With your back to the house, looking out to the car park, follow the path to your left, around the side of the house. Walk down and take the second right. Stop here and enjoy the view.

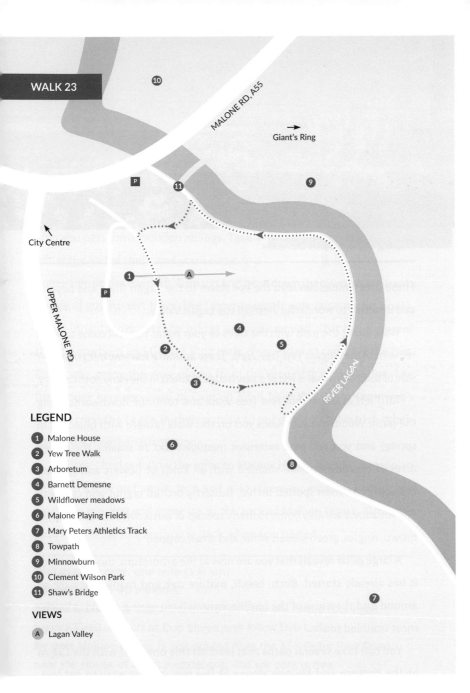

WALK 23

MALONE RD, A55

→ Giant's Ring

City Centre

UPPER MALONE RD

RIVER LAGAN

A Lagan Valley

LEGEND

1. Malone House
2. Yew Tree Walk
3. Arboretum
4. Barnett Demesne
5. Wildflower meadows
6. Malone Playing Fields
7. Mary Peters Athletics Track
8. Towpath
9. Minnowburn
10. Clement Wilson Park
11. Shaw's Bridge

VIEWS

A. Lagan Valley

24.

Sir Thomas and Lady Dixon Park

This walk takes you through Belfast's favourite park for the green fingered, with one of the world's most famous rose gardens as part of the attraction.

The son of Belfast's first Lord Mayor, Sir Thomas James Dixon was a Northern Irish senator and Lord Lieutenant of Belfast. His claim to fame, however, lies in the beautiful estate he left behind, donated to the people of Belfast in 1959 by his widow, Edith. The Sir Thomas and Lady Dixon Park might not enjoy the snappiest title, but it has become one of the city's most popular parks. Never more so than during its annual Rose Trials, when visitors from around the world converge to view the latest and best varieties around. In season, its International Rose Garden hosts many thousands of roses in bloom.

But there's more on offer than roses, as we will discover. The route we're taking tries to take advantage of the longer (yellow marked)

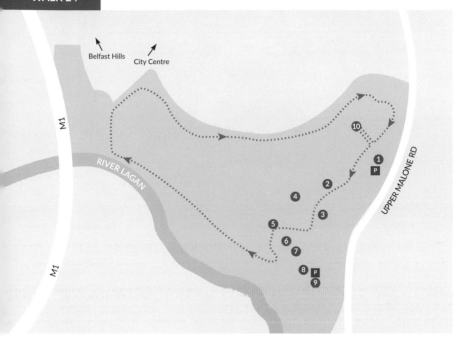

LEGEND

1. Upper Car Park – Start and finish
2. Japanese Gardens
3. Wilmont House
4. Historic Rose Gardens
5. Golden Crown Fountain
6. Victorian walled garden
7. Azalea Walk
8. Stables Cafe
9. Lower Car Park
10. International Rose Gardens

The relaxing Japanese Gardens at Sir Thomas and Lady Dixon Park.

Woodland Trail and the best of the orange Garden Trail. This way we can enjoy more of the park's 128 acres of meadows, woodland and gardens, while not missing its major attractions.

Most of the time we will follow the Woodland Trail, but to ensure that we visit the main points of interest too, we will take a detour around part of the Garden Trail to take in the Japanese Gardens, walled garden, Wilmont House and, of course, the Rose Garden.

If you're coming from the main Lagan Towpath Walk, a path takes you to the lower car park. If that is your route just walk the relatively short distance to the upper cark park, our start. If coming by car, take the second entrance from the Upper Malone Road and park in the upper car park.

Near the top of the car park you will see a gateway and, on the other side of the path, a series of wooden finger-posts. One directs you towards the international rose garden straight ahead, but we are leaving that until last and will instead turn left here.

Keep walking down in the direction of Wilmont House. Not too far along you will notice an entrance to a series of steps on your right. Marked by two solid logs on each side of the pathway and two stone pillars at the entrance, these terraced steps lead down to the charming Japanese Gardens, with their pond and Japanese bonsai trees. Spend a reflective moment or two here before returning to the path.

You're just around the corner from Wilmont House, which will soon appear on your left. Needless to say, given the territory, there is a linen connection to the estate. The area was landscaped in the mid-eighteenth century by a Scottish family, the Stewarts. Known as the Wilmont Estate, it was used, among other things, for bleaching linen. Wilmont House, a large and impressive red-brick house (not open to the public), was built in 1859 for the then owners, the Bristow family. The estate's last owners, the Dixons, bought it in 1919. US soldiers were stationed here during the Second World War (over 250,000 were positioned around Northern Ireland during the war) and the officers were billeted in Wilmont House.

To your right, over an expanse of grass, is a series of historic rose gardens, which take you around the roses of the world. Certainly worth a detour for rose lovers.

Otherwise, continue on the path, following the orange signs, and take a right turn at the T-junction. Walk along this narrow path enclosed by high hedgerows. At the Golden Crown Fountain, commissioned for the Queen's Golden Jubilee, turn left and explore the walled garden before returning via the same door. It's another meditative spot to sit on a bench on a summer's day, enjoying the charming Victorian garden.

Back out, take the path around the exterior of the walled garden and walk down. You will come to a post numbered 33. An arrow suggests a left turn towards the nearby Azalea Walk. No harm in taking a detour here,

Woodland Trail through Sir Thomas and Lady Dixon Park.

but otherwise instead turn directly right. You are now walking 'backwards' along the Woodland Trail, so don't be alarmed by yellow arrows pointing in the wrong direction as you continue.

For a while you walk with the Lagan on your left and wildflower meadows to your right. The latter are quite uneven and occasionally hilly, but worth exploring if you have time. Otherwise continue for a while. You will eventually come to a bridge and then a fork in the route. The right-hand path, marked 17, takes you a shorter route back. We bear left still along the Woodland Trail. At No. 16, turn right to follow the yellow trail. The meadows will be to your left, the woodland to your right. At 15, turn left, ignoring the arrow suggesting a right turn. The road curves around through meadows and woodland and you will get your first glimpses of the pagodas and circular wooden terraces of the International Rose Garden. However, no access is available at this point. Again, don't be deterred by arrows pointing in the other direction; we are still walking against the grain.

The path winds its way back to the upper car park, where the finger-post will point you to the International Rose Garden, now just around the corner.

If you want to relax over a snack or coffee after your walk, take yourself off to the Stables café in the lower car park.

Distance: 4 km (2.8 miles)

Average time: 80 minutes

Public transport: Metro 8A, 8B, 8C from City Hall (Donegall Square East). Get off at the junction of Upper Malone Road and Finaghy Road South: walk along the Upper Malone Road for one mile (1.6 km) to the start of the route. Ulsterbus service 524 and 524a to Drumbeg from Europa Bus Station.

By car: Take second entrance, signposted off the Upper Malone Road.

Turn into Alfred Street and walk down to St Malachy's Church. Designed by Thomas Jackson, it is probably the most beautiful in Belfast. It was initially conceived as a cathedral with room for over 7000 worshippers, but a subsequent lack of funding downsized the ambition of its driving force, Bishop Denvir, before its completion in 1844. Even so, it is regarded as one of the finest examples of Georgian architecture in Ireland, and its remarkable fan-vaulted ceiling, inspired by the Henry VII Chapel in Westminster Abbey, is a major attraction for visitors. Greatly admired by both Sir Benjamin Britten and Sir John Betjeman, its multi-million-pound restoration in 2009 included the renovation of the famous ceiling.

From St Malachy's turn right into Alfred Street, then take the second right into Sussex Place. At the corner of Sussex Place and Joy Street, adjoining the Convent of Mercy, is the former St Malachy's National School, which was built in 1878 for the children of the Markets area. This area, divided between wealthy and poorer districts, grew up around the various markets that existed around the location of today's St George's Market, virtually from Belfast's inception as a town.

Some of Belfast's most attractive Georgian and early Victorian houses can be found in Joy Street. Visitors to these houses, which were once used as theatrical lodgings, included the many stars appearing on Belfast's thriving music hall scene. Charlie Chaplin once stayed at No. 24, the boarding house of Jane O'Neill. As Joy Street's fortunes declined it became known as the 'Street of P's – Pride, Poverty and Pianos'.

Walk across Joy Street down Hamilton Street, named after James Hamilton, the man who built much of the more genteel parts of the Markets area, including the first house in the area, No. 3 Hamilton Street, in 1818. Walk to the end of Hamilton Street and turn left into Cromac Street. Cross over at the lights to Forsyth House and walk up East Bridge Street

Shopping for fish, freshly caught in the Irish Sea, at St George's Market
– Ireland's oldest covered market

to the main entrance of St George's Market where the statue of Alec the
Duck and his friend stands. Back in the 1920s, the real Alec (actually a
goose) was legendary for escorting schoolchildren across the road and,
allegedly, enjoying a drink in local pubs.

If you're here on a Friday, Saturday or Sunday during market hours you
can take a dander through Ireland's oldest covered market (see Cathedral
Quarter walk). Otherwise walk up to the lights at the junction of East Bridge
Street and Oxford Street and cross over to the other side of East Bridge Street
to walk back in the direction you came. Walk on the pathway by the houses
around the corner until you come to a house at the end of the car park with
a large mural on its gable wall. This is one of a series of murals reflecting the
heritage of the Markets area, which were developed by the local community
with Belfast-based artist Raymond Henshaw. Here you will be reacquainted
with Alec the Duck and other famous characters of the Markets.

At the junction with Ormeau Avenue, where Cromac Street becomes the Ormeau Road, turn left into Cromac Place. Now reinvented as a business park, this was the site of the old Gasworks which supplied Belfast with gas from the 1820s to the 1980s and helped power the city's transformation into an industrial giant. Over 2000 people worked here at one point, the blackened faces of workers emerging from their shifts a familiar sight for generations.

As you walk through, look to the right, where one of the most famous features of the old Gasworks stands, the old clock tower. Check out the water features outside the Radisson Blu hotel as you pass too. There were once two great gas towers here.

Just after the Lloyd's Banking Group building pass under the railway bridge and turn right, stopping when you come to the white lock-keeper's house by McConnell's Weir, overlooking the Lagan Canal. Many lock-keepers were employed on the Lagan Canal. As well as passing the lighters through the locks, their role was to maintain water levels and look after the locks. In return they were given a house to live in, like this one, and usually a vegetable garden.

You are now on the Lagan Towpath, which takes the walker from the heart of Belfast to the countryside. The towpath forms part of the Ulster Way, a 560-mile route around the province of Ulster. If you had looked out at the river a century ago, it would have been crammed with canal narrowboats and other craft carrying everything from fruit, vegetables and livestock for the markets to huge loads of coal to fire the Gasworks.

We're going to keep going along the towpath until we reach the Ormeau Bridge. If you want to take a detour into the Lower Ormeau, now largely a Catholic area, the Irish language centre, An Droichead on Cooke Street is worth a visit, as is the atmospheric Hatfield House, an attractive traditional bar with *Titanic* connections on the Ormeau Road.

Belfast Marathon
runners entering
Ormeau Park.

Though the distinction is becoming increasingly blurred, by and large the Ormeau Bridge marks the division between nationalist and unionist areas, with unionists being more plentiful on the Upper Ormeau Road. Turn left after you cross the bridge and walk along the embankment to the car park beside the Indoor Tennis Centre and Ozone Complex.

Opened in 1871, Ormeau Park was the first public park in the city and was a godsend for the people who were most responsible for Belfast's industrial success, its very badly paid workers. For these people life couldn't have been harder, working six days a week, often in the harshest of conditions. But, on Saturday afternoons and Sundays, one avenue of escape was at hand, at what became known as the 'People's Park'. They would enjoy strolling or cycling the tree-lined walks in a rural idyll a world away from their working environment. It remains one of Belfast's most popular parks to this day, not least for its sporting facilities and ecotrails.

Take the tree-lined path to the right of the centre and pass the all-weather pitches. Continue along this path past mature trees and woodland copses. Take a right at the crossroads. You will pass the former Superintendent's House within a garden on your left. Take the next right and follow the road around to the main road, Ormeau Road. Turn right, crossing the bridge. You can now retrace your steps or take public transport back to the City Centre.

Distance: 2.3 km (1.4 miles) one way
Average time: 80 minutes
Starts at: City Hall

Summary of walks

Walk	Distance	Approximate time (hours)
1. Lagan Towpath main walk	15.4 km (9.6 miles)	3–3.5
2. Lagan Towpath (Stranmillis to the Odyssey)	4.3 km (2.7 miles)	1.5
3. Cave Hill Country Park	7 km (4.3 miles)	2
4. Colin Glen Forest Park	7.2 km (4.5 miles)	1.5
5. Yardmen and Narnia	3.2 km (2 miles)	1.5
6. Divis and Black Mountain	6.8 km (4.2 miles)	2–2.5
7. Carnmoney Hill	1.5 km (1 mile)	Less than 1
8. In the footsteps of Van the Man	3 km (1.9 miles)	1.5
9. Georgie Best and river walks	6 km (3.7 miles)	2
10. The Bog Meadows	1.7 km (1.1 miles)	Less than 1
11. Cregagh Glen	2 km (1.2 miles)	1.5
12. Shankill	3.2 km (2 miles)	1.5
13. Titanic Quarter	2 km (1.2 miles)	1
14. North Belfast	3.2 km (2 miles)	1.5
15. Belfast City Cemetery	1.9 km (1.2 miles)	Variable
16. The Falls Road	4 km (2.5 miles)	1.5
17. *Titanic* and Sailortown	4 km (2.5 miles)	1.5
18. City Hall to Queen's Quarter	2.4 km (1.5 miles)	1.5
19. City Hall to Cathedral Quarter	1.9 km (1.2 miles)	1
20. Stormont Estate	4 km (2.5 miles)	1.3
21. Minnowburn and the Giant's Ring	3.4 km (2.1 miles)	1
22. Belvoir Forest Park	2.3 km (1.4 miles)	Less than 1
23. Barnett Demesne	1.6 km (1 mile)	Less than 1
24. Sir Thomas and Lady Dixon Park	4 km (2.5 miles)	1.3
25. City Hall to Ormeau Park	2.3 km (1.4 miles)	1.3

Other books from The O'Brien Press

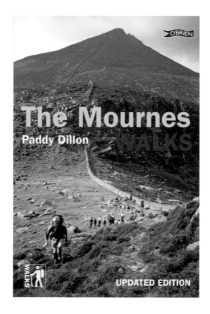

Where the mountains of Mourne sweep down to the sea

They sweep down to the sea, they rise in huge heathery humps, surrounded by farmlands divided into tiny, stone-walled fields. Explore the Mournes in the company of walking expert Paddy Dillon, taking in rugged coast, high mountains and forest parks.

Follow the mighty Mourne Wall on its meanderings and visit the quiet corners where the history, heritage, wildlife and stillness of the area can be enjoyed.

Covers all parts of the Mournes – the High and Low Mournes as well as the Kingdom of Mourne; the Silent Valley circuit; the Mourne Coastal Path; the old smuggling route of the Brandy Pad; Warrenpoint and Rostrevor; the complete Mourne Wall circuit; the Mourne Trail section of the Ulster Way in four parts from Newry to Clough; Tollymore and Castlewellan Forest Parks; as well as lesser-known outlying trails such as the Castlewellan Loanans.

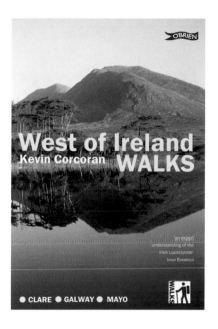

Explore the counties of Clare, Galway and Mayo in the company of a wildlife expert.

The West of Ireland offers a huge choice of landscape to the walker – mountain peaks, woodland, bogs and lakes, sandy beaches and the strange limestone plateaux of the Burren.

The walks

Clare: The Cliffs of Moher ● The Burren: Sliabh Eilbhe ● Blackhead ● Abbey Hill

Galway/Connemara: Inishmore, Aran Islands ● Casla Bog ● Errisbeg Mountains (Roundstone) ● Maumturk Mountains ● Kylemore Abbey ● Killary Harbour

Mayo: Cong ● Lough Nadirkmore (Party Mountains) ● Tonakeera Point ● Crough Patrick.

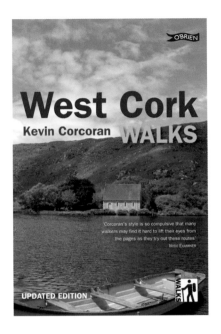

Experience the rugged wildness of Ireland's most southerly, and often considered most beautiful region, in the company of an expert naturalist. Walking in West Cork offers an incredible variety of landscape – mountainous peaks, rolling heaths, forested valleys, pristine lakes and sandy beaches – the choice is yours.

West Cork Walks details ten different walks spread across West Cork, including maps for each walk, the approximate length of time they should take, equipment required, notable features along the way and beautiful wildlife illustrations by the author. Casual strollers, family groups, ramblers and serious walkers are all catered for.

The walks: The Gearagh (near Macroom), Ballyvourney, Gougane Barra, Bere Island, Castlefreke (near Rosscarbery), Lough Hyne (near Skibbereen), Mizen Head, Priest's Leap (near Glengarriff), Glengarriff and Allihies.

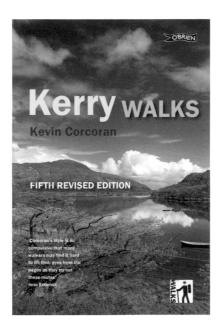

The perfect walking guide to the wildness and beauty of Kerry. Discover the landscape and wildlife of Ireland's most spectacular county with walking enthusiast and expert naturalist Kevin Corcoran. Twenty walks exploring heathland and bog, Ireland's highest mountains, coastal peninsulas, beaches, islands, forests, rivers and lakes.

Twenty walks, spread throughout the county, from four hours to eight hours, graded from casual to tough.
Clear, detailed instructions and maps.
Beautiful wildlife illustrations by the author, and information on flora and fauna.
A special Killarney section.

The walks: Lough Acoose, Bray Head, Lough Currane, Derrynane, Rossbeigh, Anascaul, Ballydavid, Great Blasket Island, Mount Eagle, The Magharees, Kenmare Uplands, Barraboy Ridge.
Killarney walks: Muckross, The Paps, Mangerton, Torc Mountain, Knockreer, Old Kenmare Road, Crohane, Tomies Wood.